THE ANSWER

STOCKHOLM TEXT

THE ANSWER

Egil Linge
Dan Josefsson

TRANSLATED BY PAUL NORLÉN

Stockholm Text
stockholm@stockholmtext.com
www.stockholmtext.com

Stockholm Text, Stockholm 2014
© 2010, 2014 Egil Linge, Dan Josefsson
by agreement with Nordin Agency
Original title: Hemligheten
Translation: Paul Norlén
Cover: Simon Svéd after
original by Niklas Lindblad
ISBN: 978-91-87441-96-7

We may be through with the past, but the past ain't through with us.

— Dr. Bergen Evans (quoted in P. T. Anderson's film *Magnolia*)

CONTENTS

EGIL'S PREFACE

For many years I had the privilege of having Carlo Perris as a mentor. He was a professor of psychiatry at Umeå University and in the early 1980s introduced cognitive therapy to Sweden. Thanks to our collaboration, I had the opportunity to be actively involved in developing this now-dominant form of therapy, both in Sweden and internationally. Cognitive psychotherapy looks at the various ways we process information and, on this basis, how we construct our reality. Or as the Greek philosopher Epictetus (ca 55-135 CE) expressed it: "It is not the events that worry us, but rather how we perceive those events." This applies not least to our way of handling relationships and intimacy.

A small child will not survive without concern and love, and the human race would not endure if we as adults could not relate to one another. This means that many people suffer when relationships don't function. Nothing arouses as many emotions as losing a close relationship, or forming a new one. In order to truly be able to experience life, we must be able to establish close relationships.

Many times as a therapist I have noticed that clients think change is a difficult, complicated process that takes endless amounts of time. But actually we all know that particular, small events can change our entire life. If we take a different way home from work, our life may take a new direction depending on what happens along the way and what people we encounter. We can call that fate or coincidence. The decisive thing, however, is how we handle these events. If we are open to change and are prepared to be present in the now, then many of these coincidences are going to enrich our lives. Otherwise they pass us by.

During my now almost thirty years as a psychologist and psychotherapist, I have had the privilege to meet amazing people and hear unique life stories. Together with my clients I have developed and tested a number of different tools that have helped people get closer to one another. I know that change is possible.

When I met Dan, I met a person who, like so many others, was trying to convince himself that loneliness was the best solution, because relationships only created problems and sometimes undesired emotions. This turned into an amazing journey. With the help of some relatively simply tools, Dan made great changes in his life.

In this book, along with Dan, I want to give a tenable explanation of what happens when relationships begin. I also want to share my therapeutic tools, which I know can help you make changes in your life.

Egil Linge

DAN'S PREFACE

Four years ago I decided to see a psychologist. I was single again after a one-year relationship and I felt empty. I'd turned forty, and for almost fifteen years my life had mainly revolved around my work as a journalist. On that front I'd had successes, but inside me there was a growing insight that I was missing out on other important aspects of life. I'd had many relationships over the years, including some that lasted a while. But it was as though I could never really be part of those relationships. Often I made myself absent by letting myself be consumed by work. I also often wondered whether I'd really met the right person and whether I was really in love. Of course this was intolerable for the one I was with, and the relationship always ended.

For a long time I believed that life had to be like this for me. I defined myself as a lone wolf, and tried to see this as unproblematic. But the prospect of getting old and becoming some kind of lonely workaholic frightened me, and there didn't seem to be any prospects for improvement. It became more and more difficult for me to get new relationships going, because the project seemed hopeless. When yet another relationship capsized, I started looking for a psychologist. I wanted help in changing my work situation. I saw that as the source of my problems.

Through a friend I made contact with Egil Linge, a psychologist and psychotherapist with almost thirty years experience in cognitive therapy. We met and I explained that I wanted to learn how to work less. Soon, however, the conversation took a new direction. Egil asked me if I really wasn't a pretty lonely guy. To my great surprise, that question made me start to cry.

I went to Egil once a week for six months, and this changed my life. During therapy, many of the ideas I'd had about how I function personally were overturned. In no way was I a lone wolf who did best on his own. On the contrary, my whole life I had been longing for intimacy. But at the same time this intimacy frightened me to such an extent that I built up a solitary life to avoid being afraid.

Egil helped me understand what emotions I often avoided by keeping myself away from a close, lasting relationship. The process was one of the most exciting I've ever been involved in. He also gave me therapeutic tools that helped me change my existence. I learned to say yes to intimacy, and at the same time was freed from a loneliness I'd carried with me as long as I can remember.

The idea of writing a book came up as the therapy was nearing its end. By then I had met my current girlfriend and said yes to her without reservations. I didn't know it then, but one year later we would have a little girl together—that too a type of undertaking I had observed with dread and skepticism my whole life. Now for the first time it felt enjoyable and important for me to have children.

At this point I realized that many of my friends were actually living with problems that resembled my own. A few of them I sent to Egil, but he couldn't take them all on. As a journalist I've always tried to write the kind of articles I want to read myself and make the kind of documentaries I myself want to see. Now I had the desire to tell as many people as possible that there were good—yes, actually scientific—explanations for why many of us have such a hard time forming close, lasting relationships. And more important: we can actually do something about the problem.

When my last session with Egil was over, he anticipated me by asking whether we shouldn't try to write a book together. Here's the book.

Dan Josefsson

CHAPTER 1:
EVERYONE NEEDS INTIMACY

In this book we're going to talk seriously about what happens when we form a relationship with someone. You are not going to be served any pick-up lines or sketches of the most strategic way to maneuver around a bar. Nor are we going to offer any tests that can help you find your dream partner (well, we are going to give you that kind of test, but it won't take very long).

What we are going to do is talk about what modern psychology knows about relationships. You're going to learn what happens inside us as human beings when a relationship begins and what causes the problems that many people have where forming relationships is concerned. We're also going to give you a set of powerful tools that can help you create the lasting relationship you want to have. These tools have been developed during many years of work with clients and are demonstrably effective.

We have two points of departure. The first is that we human beings need close, lasting relationships to feel good and to develop. From the very moment we are born, loneliness is the most frightening thing there is. As children we literally scream for intimacy. As adults we've learned to stop screaming, but that doesn't mean the need for intimacy has disappeared. Loneliness still causes us pain, simply because we are designed for a life of close interaction with others.

For a close relationship to develop, it must have some degree of permanence. Occasional encounters cannot provide the intimacy we need. Friendships are important and can be very long-lasting, but they cannot take the place of a more intimate relationship. What we need besides friends are long-term, close and loving relationships. Not necessarily life-long, but long enough so that intimacy can arise. What the relationship looks like in other respects doesn't matter. We can be homosexual, we can be heterosexual, we can have children or not, we can live in small families, in large families, in collectives or in some other arrangement. The important thing is that we allow intimacy to play a central role in our lives.

Our second point of departure is that no one really needs to live his or her life alone. This may seem like a provocative assertion, considering how common it is for modern individuals to have problems entering into long-term relationships. But it's true nevertheless. Involuntary solitude is not necessary for anyone, and we hope to convince you that this is the case.

Today more people live alone than ever before. One solution that many people are trying is searching for a partner via Internet dating or high-tech matching sites; the number of people doing this is said to be constantly increasing. This development would not have been possible if millions of people had not grown tired of loneliness.

It is also apparent that the absence of a love relationship does not say anything about an individual's other successes in life. It doesn't matter how good you look, how capable you are in your work, how well-known and respected you are or how much money you have. Involuntary loneliness strikes without respect to class background or social circumstances.

For most people, the search for a sustainable relationship involves finding the right person. This focus may seem reasonable, but it has a downside. In this book we are going to show that the problems we encounter when forming relationships exist to a great degree inside ourselves. This has been confirmed by more than forty years of psychological research, and in practice means that many of us may meet any number of potential partners who are completely "right," but without recognizing that we've just met a suitable person.

We will not solve that problem even if we scour the whole world for someone who suits us. We must first acquire knowledge of the inner mechanisms that we use to create relationships, and then find tools to fine-tune those mechanisms so they can give us the intimacy we long for. We will give you both of these things in this book.

The book is arranged so that in the first half you get knowledge about how love and relationship-formation work. This knowledge is complemented in the second half of the book by a number of tools. These have names like "do-the-opposite method," "The Car Ride," "Willingness" and "Little Person and Big Person," and are well-proven therapeutic methods for bringing about change.

A few words on gender and sexual orientation

This book includes many stories about individuals who have sought help with Egil to solve problems with involuntary solitude. So that the individuals cannot be identified, we have changed many external circumstances and sometimes even changed the person's gender. We can make such changes in identity because the problems we talk about in this book are universal. There is no difference between how men and women make a connection with other people, nor does our sexual orientation play any role in what happens inside us when we enter into an intimate relationship. So you are free to attribute the individuals in the stories your own gender and your own sexual orientation, if that makes it easier for you to identify with a certain person in the examples.

When the Relationship Won't Start

You will now meet seven individuals who have sought help from Egil with regards to starting relationships. Again, names and circumstances have been changed, but otherwise the following are authentic stories.

Matthew is never satisfied

Matthew is thirty years old and lives alone. He longs for a lasting relationship, but the ones he's been in have seldom lasted longer than a few months. Matthew is a well-liked, social person who has many friends and is successful in his work as an economist. His friends and coworkers think it's inconceivable that he has such a hard time finding someone to be with.

During the past six months, Matthew has dated a bit via the Internet. When he meets someone he likes, the first two encounters are usually fun and exciting, but around the third date his view of the partner changes.

Where before he saw a pleasant person, now serious faults began to appear. One had the wrong clothes. Another knew too little about art, and a third had the wrong political opinions. So when the suggestion to meet again comes up, Matthew backs out. By that time he's convinced that a relationship wouldn't work anyway. At the same time, he naturally sees a pattern emerge: No one is good enough.

Lately he has started to wonder whether he's simply more particular where relationships are concerned than his friends who are in relationships. In darker moments, he wonders whether there's something wrong with him personally. Matthew doesn't know what he should do to change the situation.

Maria is perfect

Maria is forty-four years old and single. She is a very social person with a job that allows her to meet a lot of people. She's content with that.

Maria has had many relationships, several of them long-term. The problem is that these relationships always, as she puts it, "seem to run out in the sand." A typical relationship for her is initially amazing, with lots of love and intimacy. Maria is an expert at getting others to feel good and has sometimes heard that she's the perfect girlfriend.

But over time the relationship becomes distant. It's as if her partner gets tired of her. This causes Maria to do her utmost so that he will feel good. But the distance only increases, and at last the relationship comes to an end. In a few cases it has turned out that the man has been unfaithful.

Maria's own theory about what causes her problem is that for some reason she falls in love with men who aren't really in love with her. However, she doesn't know why this is so or what she should do about it. Now she is often depressed and afraid to try again. At the same time she feels lonely.

Johan is in constant doubt

Johan is thirty-five years old and has had several relationships that lasted from a few months to one year. He has no major problems initiating relationships. Johan's problem is that even in a rather long-term relationship, he can't stop doubting that he's with the right person. He constantly wonders whether maybe there's someone out there who suits him better and whether he's truly in love. If he passes an interesting girl on the sidewalk, he questions his feelings for his girlfriend. If he'd really been in love, he thinks, would he be looking at other girls?

Johan lets time pass without definitively being able to say yes to his partner, and he avoids planning for the future. In time this becomes so trying for his partner that the relationship ends. Johan, however, does not want to live alone and the past year he has seriously started to worry that perhaps he will never find anyone he can stay with.

Lena wants guarantees

Lena is thirty-four years old. She works as an art director at an advertising agency and is successful. Lena has had quite a few relationships and always goes into them with great passion. She gets jealous easily and needs to feel strong acknowledgment from her partner in order to feel good. In several previous relationships she has been criticized for being clingy and demanding, and has therefore learned to restrain herself to a certain extent so as not to scare men away. Inside herself, however, she is often worried about being abandoned.

In recent years Lena has started longing to have children. In her two most recent relationships she wanted to know at a rather early stage whether or not the guy could imagine having children with her. This led to conflicts, and she was accused of making ultimatums. Both of those relationships came to an end.

Now Lena is afraid to start anything new. She feels that the risk that she will be abandoned increases the more she shows her needs. She feels truly afraid of falling in love again.

Gustav goes home before dawn

Gustav is thirty-eight years old. He has a good job that he's happy with and where he is appreciated. Gustav lives alone, but during the past twelve or thirteen years he has had over a hundred sexual interactions and brief relationships. Most often they have lasted between a day and a few weeks, and in a few cases, for two or three months. It's almost always Gustav himself who withdraws, with a feeling of being trapped and bored.

Now, however, Gustav has started to feel that life is empty and that he's tired of the endless single life. He's afraid of becoming a pathetic barfly who, as he gets older, has a harder and harder time getting a response. Gustav dreams of a stable relationship but doesn't understand how he will ever be able to start one. He often can't even manage to stay until morning with the person he goes home with. He sees no way out and feels less and less desire even for his usual one-night stands. Sometimes he wonders whether it's not just as well to accept that he's going to be alone for the rest of his life.

Beatrice is drawn to unavailable men

Beatrice is thirty-eight years old and works as a real estate agent. She has always thought relationships should be very passionate. During the past few years she has almost exclusively been interested in men who already have a wife and children. There she's found the passion she sought, but at the same time realized that an unavailable man can't give her the lasting intimacy she longs for. She has often felt frustrated by being the mistress, because she views this as demeaning. But finding someone who is not attached and still sufficiently exciting seems almost hopeless. All the available men Beatrice meets bore her to such an extent that any idea of a relationship seems impossible. Most recently she has been worried that she won't find anyone to have children with, and that soon it will be too late.

Marcus feels uncomfortable

Marcus is twenty-seven years old and works as a computer consultant. He lives alone, but would like to be in a relationship. He is well-liked among his friends, who can't understand why he has such a hard time meeting someone.

Marcus describes himself as a social person, but with poor self-esteem where women are concerned. If he meets someone in a social situation that he thinks is nice, then he usually feels rather relaxed, initially. But if the woman shows an interest in him, he gets stressed and feels more and more uncomfortable and uncertain. Such encounters end with him acting unresponsive or excusing himself and going home. Afterwards he feels relieved at getting to be by himself again, but the next day he regrets it.

Recently he has started avoiding parties and other occasions where there are women he doesn't already know. With these women, he figures, he already knows how things are going to end. He just can't cope with the thought of more failures.

The Relationship Staircase

Difficulties in creating lasting relationships can manifest themselves in many ways, and the stories about Matthew, Maria, Johan, Lena, Gustav, Beatrice and Marcus are just a few examples. Under the surface, however, almost all relationship problems have some very common denominators.

Creating a lasting relationship means that each of us, together with a strange person, gradually transforms distance and lack of familiarity into intimacy and commonality. This process can be visualized as a staircase, where each step means greater intimacy. Let's look at the process of moving to the top of the Relationship Staircase.

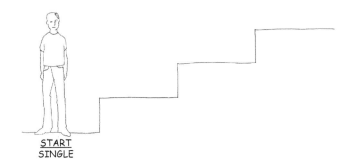

START
SINGLE

Figure 1. The Relationship Staircase: The starting point is at the foot of the staircase.

The Base of the Staircase

You start your journey alone in front of the staircase, when you are single and not dating anyone (Figure 1).

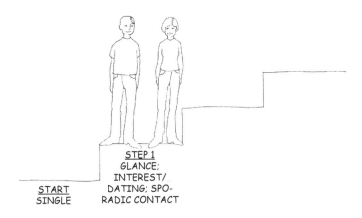

STEP 1
GLANCE;
INTEREST/
DATING; SPO-
RADIC CONTACT

START
SINGLE

Figure 2. The Relationship Staircase: The First Step.

The First Step

Generally, you stride toward the first step by meeting someone who arouses your interest (Figure 2). The two of you are strangers to each other and lack strong emotional attachments. You socialize more or less sporadically. Over time you get to know one another a little better, and realize that you want to continue to see each other regularly. This means you move up to the second step.

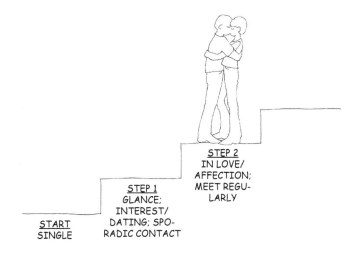

Figure 3. The Relationship Staircase. The Second Step.

The Second Step

Now you are in love and officially a couple (Figure 3). You socialize regularly and create a more and more complex picture of one another. The relationship is marked by a sense of discovery. You are in the process of finding out whether you want to invest in creating a more lasting relationship. Some couples may already move in together at this stage, but in such cases the testing nevertheless continues. Sooner or later, you know it is time to unconditionally say yes to one another and to the relationship. At that moment you move to the third step.

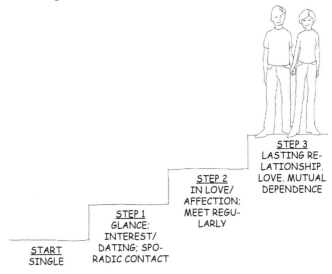

Figure 4. The Relationship Staircase: The Third Step.

The Third Step
Now you promise one another lasting intimacy (Figure 4). This means that you can relax in a way that is often not possible on Steps One and Two. You have become each other's secure reference points in existence. As of now, it is difficult to imagine life without the other. You have created an intimate, lasting relationship.

26

On a superficial level, the movement on the staircase may appear completely different, depending on which people are involved. A Swedish couple who meet one another at work will probably use different rituals to get closer to one another than a couple who lives in a war-ravaged country and happen to meet in a bomb shelter. Two eighteen-year-olds will engage in different activities as they develop their relationship than a middle-aged couple might. Each sequence of events is unique. But under the surface, all relationships develop according to the patterns we have described above.

Climbing the staircase can go quickly or take a long time, depending on who is making the journey. It may happen that two strangers fall in love with one another and immediately agree that they want to spend many years together. They may then pass the second step in a short time and quickly move to the third. In order for this to work, however, the parties must emotionally move in tempo with each other in a way that is largely unusual.

There are also examples of two individuals who socialize in the same circles for years before one day they fall in love with each other and move in together. Such a relationship moves in slow motion from the first step (the first encounters) to the second (in the form of friendship), but then stops there. The two involved may not know it themselves, but now a long period of testing ensues where they, as friends, get to see enough sides of each other that intimacy can arise. One day, all that is needed is a late-blooming attraction and then the relationship finds itself on the third step.

Why do we get stuck on the staircase?

If you ask Matthew, Maria, Johan and the others why

they are single even though they don't want to be, several of them will answer that they simply haven't had the good luck to meet the right partner yet. This is a pretty common idea and it means that there isn't much more to do about involuntary solitude than keeping your fingers crossed. But fortunately this is not true. Their problems are rather that they all have difficulties in moving up the Relationship Staircase, and everything that goes along with being open to increased intimacy.

Some make their way again and again to the first step with various partners but get no further. Others get stuck on the second step and can't make their way to the third step. There are those who attempt to force a relationship to the third step without passing the testing period on Step Two. And then there are those who don't step onto the staircase at all, because (they think) they have never meet anyone to try with. The variations are many, and we will be talking more about them later on in this book.

What we will do now is ask why these problems arise at all. How is it that some people apparently easily make their way up this staircase and settle down at the top, while others again and again get stuck or stumble and fall? This is a question that can actually be answered.

Love and Theories

During the past sixty years, extensive psychological research has been done about how children form relationships. This research has in turn led, in the past ten or fifteen years, to much new knowledge about how adult relationships function. For that reason, today we know in what way an individual's inner prerequisites for creating intimacy differ, what causes these differences, and what can be done about it.

All this knowledge is gathered in a psychological theory called attachment theory, and interest in this theory is currently growing quickly among researchers, psychologists and psychotherapists. This is understandable, because attachment theory provides answers to questions that people have wondered about from time immemorial. For example, why loneliness causes us human beings to feel so bad and why some people seemingly casually enter into relationships and stay there for decades, while others don't succeed in keeping a relationship together longer than a few weeks. Attachment theory explains why people experience love and attraction so differently, and why some people seem to be drawn to one another as if by an invisible force. And it explains what happens when an attraction turns into a lasting relationship and why this process sometimes goes wrong.

Thanks to attachment theory we no longer need to refer to fate when we have a hard time finding someone to be together with. Involuntary solitude has more concrete explanations than that, and thus there are also better solutions than simply hoping for the best.

We will soon say more about attachment theory, but first we want to say a few words about what psychological theories are—and what they are not. Psychological theories basically function just like theories in the natural sciences like physics and chemistry. They are always about finding various types of connections. Take Newton, for example. He discovered a connection between the size of the planets and how strongly they were attracted to each other. His hypothetical theory eventually became the Law of Gravitation, and with that he could explain why the moon orbits the earth and why an apple falls to the ground. In the same way, the field of psychology tries to find connections between various factors in individual lives. These connections are collected in theories, with whose help we can explain the kind of behaviors we did not previously understand.

It is more difficult, however, to study human beings than falling apples. You, the reader of this book, are the product of a nearly infinite number of factors. You are a mental being and have gathered mass quantities of experiences that influence what you think, feel and do. In order to explain who you are, it must therefore be known what you have previously experienced, including the sort of experiences you yourself don't remember. At the same time you are a social being who is constantly changing and developing through interaction with other people. This means that it really shouldn't be possible to understand who you are without also knowing how the people around you function. Finally, you are an extremely complicated biological organism who is influenced by both the physical environment in which you live and your genetic makeup, so you are affected mentally and physically by the present as well as how your past relatives functioned.

Finding connections in this muddle that can explain why we function as we do isn't easy. But it can be done. However different we may seem, there are many mechanisms that unite us if we just dig a little deeper inside.

Attachment theory is the result of sixty years of research into how human relationships function. By studying children and adults it has been possible to map out many of the factors that come into play when we human beings try to make emotional attachments with one another.

Attachment theory is based on dividing people into various groups based on what problems they have as far as relationships are concerned. These group divisions are a good way to visualize the various connections upon which the theory is based, but at the same time the classifications are a simplification of reality. If you sometimes feel you function differently than what the theory maintains, you're very likely right. Individuals are always much more multifaceted than any existing theories about them. But you will still benefit from the picture attachment theory paints of how a human being generally functions.

Attachment theory in a nutshell

Attachment theory is based on the discovery that we humans learn to create relationships when we are very young. We use the knowledge we acquire early on about how relationships function for the rest of our lives. When you meet someone you like, then you use—without knowing it—approximately the same behaviors to create intimacy with that person as you did with your parents or guardians when you were little.

This means that the quality of the relationship that we had once upon a time with our parents plays an important role in how easy or difficult it is for the rest of our lives to create intimacy with others. With gross simplification, human beings can be divided into two groups. In one group are those whose experiences during childhood made them secure in their relationships.

In the other group are those whose experiences made them insecure. Those who belong to the secure group have a relatively easy time finding someone to be with. Those who belong to the insecure group have a more difficult time. Here we find Matthew, Maria, Johan and all the others who think that relationships are pretty tricky.

The insecure group can in turn be roughly divided into two subgroups: the insecure-avoidant group and the insecure-ambivalent group. These terms can be a little complicated at the beginning, but we'll carefully explain what they mean.

All people thus belong to one of the following three groups:

1. The secure group
2. The insecure-avoidant group
3. The insecure-ambivalent group

How we handle our relationships depends to a great extent on which group we belong to. We will now look more closely at what characterizes the various groups. It may be the case that you recognize yourself in more than one group. This is due to the fact that many of us actually fall somewhere between the various groups. We'll return to this later.

The secure group

Individuals who belong to the secure group think it is relatively easy to get close to other people. They are seldom worried about being abandoned and do not feel very often that someone wants to get so close to them that it doesn't feel good. This group feels generally satisfied with being dependent on others and has no problems allowing others to be dependent in return. At the same time they do relatively well in their own company. They do not experience solitude as a threat, even if they most often prefer to be with others.

When they have finally entered into a relationship they are satisfied with it, and as a rule their relationships are long-term. Their friends often have a hard time even imagining them as single.

The insecure-avoidant group

Individuals in the insecure-avoidant group are often very social. They are good at dealing with people and are well-liked by those around them. Often they are careful about their appearance and like to keep their homes in order. They are usually appreciated by employers because they are often very ambitious and handle their jobs professionally.

But individuals who belong to this group do not feel really satisfied with being close to other people. They sometimes feel that others want to be more intimate than what they think feels right. Therefore they tend to maintain a certain distance in their relationships. In the introductory phase of a relationship they are careful about their integrity and do not like it when things develop too quickly. In more long-term relationships they sometimes hear that they are "too perfect" and that it is difficult to get close to them.

When they meet a potential partner and try to judge whether a relationship is worth investing in, they often try to think their way to the answer rather than investigating what they feel. They are thus governed more by thoughts than by emotions in their relationships.

Individuals in this group do not like being dependent on another person, and prefer not to see that someone else is dependent on them. They believe they manage crises better on their own than if they have to interact with someone else. When they feel pressured in connection with a relationship, they have a tendency to want to be by themselves. Sometimes they experience solitude as a nice break compared with the demands for intimacy that are often made while in a relationship.

The insecure-ambivalent group

Individuals in the insecure-ambivalent group are often perceived as creative, dynamic personalities who are very emotional. They have an easy time offering themselves and may, for example, risk telling private things about themselves, even to people they don't know particularly well.

Where relationships are concerned, this group is in many respects the opposite of the insecure-avoidant group. They like getting close to other people and are more likely to have problems with sometimes wanting more intimacy than others are prepared to give. Perhaps they have sometimes experienced that their strong desire for intimacy has frightened people away. When they try to figure out whether a partner is someone to invest in, they proceed to a great degree on how the relationship feels, rather than trying to think their way to the answer. They are thus governed more by emotions than by thoughts in relationships.

Individuals in this group experience a strong need

for their partner relatively early in a relationship. They may feel like half a person when they are alone. When they do have a relationship, they are often worried about whether the potential partner's love is sufficiently strong, and fear abandonment. It may be easy for them to become suspicious and jealous, and if the partner wants time to himself/herself, this may cause considerable anxiety. When they feel pressured and worried in a relationship they often want to have close contact with the partner (or their date, if this is a new acquaintance). They may for example want to call often, even though this may cause them to feel clingy and dependent.

In situations where they do not think they can rely on their partner, they may overcompensate by being aloof and pushing the partner away. They then feel torn, sad and perhaps angry.

Sometimes their worry about being abandoned can be so trying that they refuse to enter into relationships at all. The result is thus a self-imposed solitude.

This is a brief, simplified description of how individuals in the secure, the insecure-avoidant and the insecure-ambivalent groups function. There will be a more thorough description later.

In the next chapter we will look more closely at what experiences in your childhood determine whether you are secure in your relationships, or if you lean toward the insecure-avoidant or insecure-ambivalent direction. In order to find this out we have to go back a little in time, more precisely to the middle of the twentieth century and right after the Second World War, when attachment theory came about.

Chapter 2:

ATTACHMENT THEORY: HIDDEN MECHANISMS OF RELATIONSHIPS

Attachment theory was formulated by the British psychoanalyst and child psychiatrist John Bowlby. At first the theory had nothing to do with adult relationships; Bowlby was primarily interested in studying why children create such strong emotional bonds with their parents. The result was a theory that he continued to develop for over forty years, until his death in 1990. At that point attachment theory had gained wide acceptance among psychologists and researchers all over the world. Since then it has been developed further by other researchers, and now also explains how relations between adults function.

Shortly after the Second World War, Bowlby was commissioned by the UN World Health Organization (WHO) to investigate why children without parents function so poorly. Throughout Europe, there were many children whose parents had died in the war. They received food and shelter at orphanages, but everywhere it was reported that the children seemed to be depressed by their stay in the orphanages. Many died unaccountably, even though they did not seem to be suffering from any illnesses.

John Bowlby visited a number of orphanages and saw how the children were taken care of by a constantly changing series of attendants. No one had time to form an intimate relationship with the children, nor was this considered important—at that time it was believed that small children did not need much more than food and a warm bed in order to prosper.

John Bowlby's studies led him to the conclusion that the orphanage children were afflicted by psychological problems because they lacked intimacy. It was loneliness that was killing them.

The research results were presented in a reputable scientific journal in 1950. Bowlby's findings did not fit in at all with the psychological theories of that time, and so initially he was ridiculed and opposed. But little by little his discovery made an impact. Orphanages the world over changed their procedures, sometimes by such simple means as letting children sleep two to a bed so they could have some form of contact. The mysterious depressions and deaths largely disappeared.

Intimacy is just as important as food

Bowlby's great discovery was that children have a biological need for lasting intimacy with a small number of adults. The reason we have this need for intimacy is that we in contrast to many other animals, are born with a brain that is undeveloped in many respects. In order for us to develop the capacity to handle thoughts and emotions, there must be a close interplay with parents and/or other nearby adults. Without that intimacy we cannot develop into functioning people.

Human children are much more defenseless when they are born compared to most other animals. Many animals can flee from enemies and search for food themselves almost immediately after birth, but as infants we humans have no chance of surviving on our own. Humans are therefore born with the instinct to try to get close to adult protectors. The feeling of being carried and of lying near a parent's warm body signals to us that we are being taken care of and protected. But if we are forced to be alone for long periods, we risk becoming ill, both mentally and physically.

Over the years Bowlby made many sensational discoveries about how children and their parents build up their relationships. He showed that newborn children do not simply wait passively to be taken care of, as was previously believed. Instead, we human beings are experts at actively initiating lasting relationships from the moment we are born—all in order to increase our chances of surviving and developing.

The first thing we do in the minutes after birth, after we have taken our first few breaths, is to look around for someone to start an intimate relationship with. If there is anyone at hand who can meet our gaze, we look him or her deeply in the eyes. Anyone who has ever experienced this first glance from a newborn child knows that it is a magical experience. There's no way to understand how a little person who just started breathing, who is exhausted after childbirth and who has never before seen another person, can nevertheless lie there and transfix an adult with its gaze. This glance is the child's way of actively starting its very first lasting relationship.

Adult love is childish

During our first few years of life, we use a series of advanced methods to get our parents and other adults to form strong emotional bonds with us. We continue to use some of these techniques throughout life when we want to approach a partner to initiate a love relationship. The majority of behaviors that we think are part of adult love we actually already mastered as three-year-olds. Let's look at some examples.

A one-year-old can enchant its parents and other adults through its frank way of seeking eye contact and smiling. It almost seems as if the child is flirting with its surroundings. This is an innate technique for connecting to adults, who often cannot keep from smiling back. Thereby an emotional bond is created that increases the probability that the adult will be prepared to rescue the child if it is in danger.

When we as adults seek contact with a potential partner whom we have never met before, we make eye contact and smile, a technique that we fully mastered back when we were one-year-olds. If the person we are smiling at feels somewhat secure, he or she will instinctively feel acknowledged and more or less automatically smile back. The interplay that arises follows the same pattern, neurologically in our brains, as it did when we, as one-year-olds, flirted with strangers on the bus. It is thus not really the child's behavior that is reminiscent of adult flirting, but the other way around. What we call "flirting" is a technique that we have carried with us from childhood.

Another example of the connection between childhood and adult life is the intense yearning for physical intimacy that shows up when we are in love. As one-year-olds we needed to spend lots of time in our parents' secure embrace. We were fascinated by their bodies and happily played with their noses, ears and hair. When we were sad we became calm simply by getting close by them. The same needs and behaviors show up again when we are older and fall in love. We feel that we must uninterruptedly touch one another, and we often want to lie intertwined together. We are fascinated by our partner's body, his or her ears, nose, hands and hair. If we are nervous or sad, we often calm down when the other one is in proximity. There are two situations in life where we behave like this with another person: When we are very small children and when we are adults and newly in love.

Another similarity between our childhood and adulthood relationships is the need to imitate. We can imitate our parents' facial expressions and some of their body movements immediately after birth. For a long time it was believed that children did not begin to imitate their parents until they were a year old, but a few years ago a research team showed that children imitate their parents as soon as twenty minutes after birth. Imitation is a way of connecting. The parents unconsciously perceive the child's imitative behavior as a signal of belonging to them, which increases their desire to protect the child. What many do not know is that as adults in love we also imitate our partner's body movements and facial expressions. When our partner draws a hand through his or her hair or places one leg across the other, we do the same. Here too we see how behaviors from the time of infancy repeat themselves in adult life. Through imitating one another we send signals that we interpret as invitations to a deepened relationship, just like we did when we were small.

As small children we babbled and talked baby talk. Everywhere in the world, parents talk with a special, lighter voice to their small children. When we become adults and fall in love, we use the same light tone when we talk with our partner. This often occurs unconsciously. This special form of address means that the person we are talking with usually feels taken care of and secure, just like when he or she was little. Some couples in love go so far that they only talk baby talk with each other—the connection between our infancy and our adult love can hardly be clearer than that.

There are many other examples. When we're little we often think it's painful to be separated from our parents even for short periods. And when we are reunited we need to quickly climb into the parent's arms to assure ourselves that intimacy has not disappeared. In the same way, as loving adults we can feel like a few hours or a few days apart is an eternity. When we are finally reunited we feel immense happiness and want to have as much touching and acknowledgment as possible. Here too, people in love are thus functioning more or less like infants. Of course we can also feel longing for our friends, but the absence is not as intense and we therefore seldom throw ourselves into the arms of a friend who's been out of town for a week.   Another striking resemblance between the relationship-building of childhood and adult life is idealization. As children we see our parents as all-knowing and perfect. There is no limit to what we believe they can bring about. When we have become adults and fallen in love, we idealize our partner in exactly the same way. He or she is unique and infallible. When we meet friends, we tend to talk uninterruptedly about the object of our attraction. Those around us realize that there is no room for nuances, and hopefully they're tactful enough to let us be.

This idealization is inherited from childhood and helps us to connect in a short time to a person who perhaps quite recently was a stranger. In this way, a process begins that may lead to the stranger becoming closer to us than anyone else.

▶ ◀

As you see, there is a long list of similarities between how we as children connect to our parents and how we as adults connect to our partner. Flirting, wordless contact, imitation, a special loving way of talking, pain at being separated and idealization—we go through all this as children with our parents and in our adult relationships with our partners.

Of course, this does not mean that adults behave exactly like infants. An obvious difference is that adult sexuality emerges in puberty. Another difference is that when we are adults and connect to another adult, the roles are not divided up as when we were children. When you were little, you probably behaved like a child and your parents like adults. In an adult love relationship, it is rather the case that you and your partner alternatively act the "child" and "parent" with one another. If one of you feels sad, the other will take a more protective role reminiscent of a parent's during childhood. The one who feels weak is then allowed to be comforted by the other. These roles can then be exchanged as needed. This capacity to both give and receive protection is characteristic of all functioning love relationships.

Negative connections with childhood
If, for example, behavior from childhood had only re-

mained in the form of the capacity to flirt or as the desire to touch the one we're in love with, all would have been well and good. But our early experiences may also give us problems when we become adults. To what degree we have problems depends on whether or not our parents succeeded in giving us all the intimacy and security we needed. Bowlby attributes this as the parents' capacity to be the "secure base" of their child's existence.

Children can be compared to airplanes on an aircraft carrier. The plane leaves the carrier and flies out over the sea, but sooner or later it must return to the carrier to refuel, or else it will crash. In the same way, as children we need to have our parents as a secure base from which to proceed when we venture off to investigate the world. We need to feel that they encourage and are happy about our desire to discover and learn; otherwise we don't dare leave and can't develop in a good way. At regular intervals we must then return to the base to fill up our supply of security. In such situations we must be absolutely certain that our parents are truly there for us. The greater access we have to our parents' intimacy and protection, the easier it is for us to develop into secure people and the easier it will be for us to create our own intimate relationships when we become adults.

Being born is like playing the lottery. We can't choose our parents. The possibility exists that we'll get parents who succeed in being a secure base in our existence, but naturally, nothing is certain. Some parents have lots of patience; others get tired more quickly. Some are good at handling emotions and intimacy, while others have a harder time with showing feelings. Some can deal with their children making demands on them; others become easily frustrated. Financial and social circumstances may make it difficult for parents to be as close to us as they perhaps would have wanted. There may be a long list of possible reasons that many of us did not have as secure a childhood as we really needed.

Your innate capacity for adaptation

How do children handle the fact that parents have such different qualifications for giving them the intimacy and security they need? Well, attachment research shows that children have an innate capacity to adapt their way of being so that it suits their parents' way of functioning. The purpose of this adaptation is to extract from the parents as much intimacy and protection as possible. The child thus adapts her behavior so as to maximize her chances of getting the intimacy required and thus develop in a positive way.

The first person to track this phenomenon was Mary Ainsworth, a coworker of John Bowlby. In the 1960s she developed a laboratory test with which she could demonstrate that children actually adapt to their parents. The test was called the "Strange Situation" and in time made Mary Ainsworth world-famous. The test is still used today by attachment researchers all over the world.

The Strange Situation is based on children who are just over a year old being exposed to abandonment. The purpose is to study to what degree these children are secure with their parents. In the experiment, one of the parents, together with the child, goes into a room where they have never been before. There are toys on the floor and a couch where a strange person is sitting. The whole thing is reminiscent of an ordinary waiting room, with the difference that the researchers are studying and videotaping what is happening in the room. After a while, the parent leaves the room and closes the door behind him. The child is left alone with the stranger for three minutes, then the parent comes back. This brief separation is repeated one more time, and then the test is done.

Secure children
A large group of children who are tested in the Strange Situation become surprised and sad when the parent leaves the room, and then even happier when the parent shows up again after three minutes. These children will then run to the parent's arms and clearly show that they feel secure there. Children who behave like this have lived with parents who are sensitive to their needs and have therefore become the secure base in their existence. Thus, in attachment research it is said that these children have a secure attachment to their parents.

Insecure-avoidant children
Other children react differently. One group seems not to react at all when the parent goes out the door; they neither cry nor complain. When after three minutes the parent come back, the child often does not react, neither with happiness nor in any other way. They do not want to be carried and perhaps even turn away from the parent. It sometimes appears as if the child is completely ignoring his or her parents.

An outside observer may easily believe that these children are uncommonly secure—after all, they show no signs of stress even when they are left alone in an unfamiliar environment. In reality, they are everything but secure. If you take the child's pulse and register the level of stress hormones in their saliva (which was done in connection with Ainsworth's test), you'll find that they are in a state of pure panic. Their pulse is racing and stress hormones surging, but they do not reveal this via their expressions. Even though they are only one year old, they have become experts at concealing their emotions.

The explanation is that the parents have not really been able to handle their child's need for consolation and intimacy. When the child has been sad and needed closeness, he or she has fairly consistently been rejected. The parents have demonstrated over and over again to their child that intimacy lessens if the child shows emotional needs. But each child needs lots of intimacy in order to be able to develop. Therefore, the child simply adapts his behavior so that it will not unleash his parents' rejection. He learns to conceal the kind of emotions and needs his parents cannot put up with and learns to keep his distance, all to rescue what little closeness to his parents there is a chance to get. The child stands out as unusually well adapted and independent, but is actually insecure. Within attachment research it is said that children who have adapted in this way have an insecure-avoidant attachment to their parents. This label sounds as if the child simply avoids his parents, but in reality avoidance is the only way the child has to create closeness to his unwilling parents.

Insecure-ambivalent children

A third group of children is clingy and dissatisfied even when they are entering the unfamiliar room together with their mom or dad. They cling tightly to the parents and do not want to investigate the room on their own. When after a while the parent goes toward the door, these children become extremely agitated and in tears try to make the parent stay. When the parent nonetheless goes out and closes the door behind him or her, the children become inconsolable. Perhaps they remain standing, kicking and striking at the door, or else they collapse in desperation on the floor. Sometimes the children become so disconsolate that the test must be shortened and the parent then simply stands outside the door for half a minute.

It may seem that these children ought to be extremely glad when the parent comes back, but they react neither with happiness nor with relief. The children do often signal that they want to be picked up, but once in the parent's arms they do not become calmer. They continue to scream and complain and try to wriggle down to the floor, only to want to be picked up again the next moment. Some even strike at their parents. The children are attempting to simultaneously get close to the parent and increase the distance to him or her. It is this inability to decide that provides the term insecure-ambivalent attachment to these children's relationships with their parents.

The children who belong to this group have capricious parents who can sometimes be strongly involved with their children one moment, but completely occupied by their own needs the next. The access to intimacy and security is thus governed to a large degree by the parents' needs and desire to be close to the children, not by the children's needs. The children are therefore forced to live with a constant worry that the intimacy on which they depend will be torn away from them. In order to minimize this risk they have adapted their behavior. Through constantly being clingy and demanding, they uninterruptedly remind their self-centered parents that they exist. This adaptation means that the children get a little more intimacy than they would have if they had been silent and obedient. However, they seldom feel calm because they know that their parents cannot be relied upon. Suspiciously they watch every step the parents take.

▶ ◀

To recap, when investigating how one-year-olds have adapted to their parents, there are three variations. The children may have created:

- a secure attachment
- an insecure-avoidant attachment
- an insecure-ambivalent attachment.

Among all children who have been investigated in the Western world, 60-70% are secure, 15-25% insecure-avoidant, and 5-15% insecure-ambivalent.

Childhood and adult life are connected
We have previously stated that adults can deal with relationships in three different ways: They may belong to the secure group, the insecure-avoidant group or the insecure-ambivalent group. These groups are the same for children and adults. Our way of adapting to our parents when we were young affects our way of handling relationships for the rest of our lives. We bring certain childhood behaviors with us into adult life.

This connection between childhood and adult life is often completely unconscious. As adults we believe that what we think, say and do in our relationships is governed by who we happen to meet, how we are doing personally and many other external circumstances. But actually the way in which we once adapted to our parents plays a decisive role in how we experience our current situation. This explains why we often may have a hard time understanding our own behavior in relationships. We are governed unconsciously by the things that happened to us many, many years earlier, things we may not even clearly recall.

The fourth type of attachment

We have now talked about three different types of connections: first, the secure attachment. Then two variations, both of which are insecure: the insecure-avoidant attachment and the insecure-ambivalent attachment. But there is also a fourth type of attachment, called insecure-disorganized. This type of attachment afflicts children who grow up under very difficult circumstances. The children are perhaps subjected to physical or mental abuse, or else their parents had such difficult experiences during their own childhood that they are not able to interpret their children's signals in a correct manner. Perhaps they often react with fury or fear when their children cry and want to be picked up. The result can be that the children are scared of their parents' reactions, though they have to attempt to connect with them anyway. Such an insoluble conflict leads to serious relationship disturbances.

People with this type of attachment often have severe relationship problems as adults and probably need more help than this kind of book can provide. We will therefore not take up disorganized attachment much in this book.

Instead we will look more closely at how the connection between childhood and adult life functions in practice.

Chapter 3:

YOUR RELATIONSHIP MODEL

Most of us don't remember much of what we experienced before the age of three. Nevertheless, attachment theory says that our way of handling relationships as adults is strongly marked by how we adapted to our parents when we were very small. The question is how we can be influenced by something that happened so early that we don't remember anything about it. To sort this out, we will have to look at how human memory functions.

In simplified terms, you might say that your brain consists of two halves. In the left half is your so-called knowledge memory, the memory you need to be able to understand words, to speak, to draw logical conclusions and to be able to recall theoretical knowledge that you acquire—for example, that Copenhagen is the capital of Denmark or that water boils at 212 degrees Fahrenheit. The right brain houses your emotions and something called your emotional memory. The emotional memory functions like a photo album. All the situations that you have ever been involved in are stored as mental images in the album, along with a memory of the emotions that the situations evoked in you. The emotional memory functions completely without words. Thus you are seldom aware of what is in the emotional memory, but it nevertheless affects you almost constantly. Thanks to the images there, you can quickly interpret complex situations and know how you ought to act. The process occurs without needing to bring your thoughts in, and often you yourself don't really understand where the knowledge comes from. Often this is called "intuition," but what has actually happened is that you unconsciously connected a certain situation to a wordless emotional memory stored in your right brain.

During our first years of life, it is the right brain that develops the fastest. Most people do not learn to talk until about the age of two because it is not until then that the left brain and the ability to speak have developed sufficiently. Our brains are actually not completely developed until we are about twenty-five.

When you were really little, the right brain was so dominant that you were almost always referred to the right brain's emotional memory when you tried to learn how the world functioned. You had almost no access to language and rational thoughts. But thanks to your emotional memory, you could still learn how to best adapt to your parents in the way we described in the last chapter.

Just like a cat that learns what behavior causes its keeper to open the refrigerator and take out food, you were forced to test your way to the kind of behaviors that led to a similar vital intimacy. When you did something that proved to increase intimacy with your parents, then an image of your actions and feelings was stored in your emotional memory's photo album. The same thing happened when you did something that reduced intimacy. Thanks to these wordless memory images, you could repeat the kinds of behavior that increased intimacy and avoid the kind that led to rejection. In that way, you efficiently researched your way to a good strategy for survival.

By the time you were about a year and a half old, your mental photo album was so full of images of the interplay with your parents that it was transformed into something that in this book we call your relationship model. The relationship model is simply a model for how, based on your previous experiences, relationships must be handled so that intimacy will be as great as possible. It consists of a large number of images in your emotional memory.

Once your relationship model had taken shape, you do not need to test your way forward in the same way as you did before. The relationship model becomes a quick guide that tells you how relationships functioned in your particular family. Above all, the relationship model includes two types of important information (Figure 5):

- A combined image of how your parents function. Can they be relied on? Are they concerned about your needs? Do they consider you valuable?
- A strategy for getting as close to your parents as possible. Do you need to conceal your emotions so as not to be rejected? Do you have to watch your parents so as not to be forgotten?

During the rest of your childhood, the relationship model guided how you handled the relationship with your parents. The guidance was strongest when you needed your parents' closeness and protection the most. Back then the relationship model dictated your behavior with such force that you reflexively did as it said. We saw examples of how that may appear in the last chapter when the children were tested in the Strange Situation—they were subjected to concern about being left alone and this led to their relationship models taking over. The result was that one child clung tight and cried, while another concealed his worry. The children got help from their relationship models and behaved in a way that maximized the chance of not being left alone.

The relationship model remains throughout life

Your relationship model does not disappear when you grow up. During your whole life it remains as part of your emotional memory. Its content, however, has changed in significant ways since you were little. The image of how your parents functioned has been transformed to your image of what you generally can expect from other people in a relationship context. In the same way, your image of the best strategy for approaching your parents has turned into a general strategy for how you ought to act when you approach a (potential) partner.

This means that your relationship model, throughout your life, influences what you feel, think and do as far as relationships are concerned. As soon as you have a chance for intimacy, the relationship model is activated and guides you. Then you "know" what you ought to do and not do. This process occurs unconsciously, in a flash, and it may lead to your acting, in relationship after relationship, in a way that you yourself have a hard time explaining.

Let's see how this might work in practice. Say that when you were little you often noticed that your parents couldn't put up with you when you were sad or angry. Perhaps they became angry themselves instead of giving you security and showing you how to handle difficult emotions. Images of countless situations when you tried to get close to your parents are stored in your relationship model. If translated into words, your relationship model would look approximately like this: "My parents are unsympathetic and can't put up with my emotions." The model may also include a good strategy for maximizing intimacy: "If I try to get close to my parents, they reject me and that hurts. If I keep my distance, they will put up with me." By means of the relationship model, you got as much intimacy as possible from your parents (see Figure 5).

When you are grown up and meet a potential partner, you still have the same relationship model you have always carried with you (see Figure 6). In principle, it includes the same image of how relationships function as it did when you were little, but the assertions about your dad, for example, have been transformed in order to deal with people in general, including your potential partner:

- Image of others: "People are unsympathetic and ungenerous."
- Strategy to create intimacy: "I have to keep my distance in order not to be rejected."

When you find yourself in a situation where there is intimacy within reach, your relationship model will be activated and to a large degree guide your experiences and actions. The result may be that your thoughts, feelings and actions suddenly change. Most of us have experienced this. One moment we feel secure and satisfied with the person with whom we're socializing—perhaps we're even becoming a little attracted and the union feels light and fun. But the next moment we're suspicious, jealous and feel the need to create distance. If someone were to ask what caused the change in outlook, we wouldn't be able to give a good answer— namely because we are not conscious of the fact that the relationship model is now guiding us, according to an old strategy we've brought with us from our childhood.

Figure 5. The Relationship Model. As a child you store two kinds of information in a separate memory: a description of how your parents function, and a strategy for how you might get as close to your parents as possible. This information becomes your relationship model, i.e. your guide to how you should best behave in order to get intimacy from your parents. As we will soon see, the relationship model follows us into adult life and influences how we handle relationships during the rest of our lives.

Figure 6. Now the child in Figure 5 has become an adult. She still has her relationship model with her from childhood. As soon as she meets someone who arouses her interest, the relationship model is activated. This then guides her expectations of the potential partner, and her way of acting in relation to him/her.

As mentioned before, our relationship model is part of our emotional memory, to which our conscious thoughts have no access. We can therefore never rationally survey and analyze in what way the relationship model takes control of us. It simply happens, and then we have about as little capacity for reflection as we had when we were a year old. Often we try, however, to construct thoughts that can make what is happening somewhat comprehensible, at least to ourselves. If the relationship model is driving us to create distance so we won't be rejected, then perhaps our conscious thoughts are saying that we've suddenly realized that the other person isn't good enough for us, that we've understood that he or she can't be relied on, or that we've simply gotten tired of the person in question. These thoughts, however, are often after-the-fact constructions. The relationship model guides us based on images that were created in our childhood, and these seldom have anything to do with our actual situation as adults. The risk therefore exists that this damages our ability to achieve intimacy. The strategies that we as children were forced to use to get close to our capricious or unsympathetic parents probably don't work just as well with people we meet as adults. But unfortunately, the relationship model doesn't take this into account. The great majority of the problems that people experience in connection with adult relationships are therefore due to the fact that our relationship models have led us completely astray.

Two friends, two images of the world

Imagine that two friends are standing in a bar. Friend A has a secure attachment style from childhood. In his/her relationship model, he or she has stored an image of other people as generous and well-intentioned, and so his/her strategy for creating intimacy is based on showing interest and getting closer.

Friend B has an insecure-avoidant attachment and in his relationship model has stored an image of others as egoistic and manipulative and a strategy for creating intimacy that is based on maintaining distance and hiding feelings.

Now Friend A and Friend B are having a beer together. Both are relaxed and think it's fun to be together. Suddenly a stranger that both of them might be interested in comes up to them and says, "Hi!" How will they react?

There is a great probability that Friend A will get to know the new acquaintance out of curiosity, while Friend B will take a more wait-and-see attitude. Friend A and Friend B will perceive the situation quite differently because their relationship models are different. For Friend A the guidance from the relationship model is no problem, because it creates openness and increased intimacy. But for Friend B the guidance is problematic. It prevents him or her from creating intimacy.

Your model is the sum of your close contacts

Up to now we have said that the relationship model is formed based on how our parents treated us when we were small. But it's actually a bit more complicated than that. If you spent a lot of time with both your dad and your mom during your first years of life, then you adapted in different ways to each one of them and in that case, two alternative strategies for creating intimacy were stored in your relationship model. It is also the case that as children we may connect to an additional two or three adults besides our parents. Perhaps we get really close to an aunt, a neighbor or a staff person at a daycare. In that case, images of how the interplay with those individuals worked are also going to affect our relationship model. Each one of us creates a unique combination of relationship experiences, and based on these experiences we form the relationship model that we will use later in life. Depending on our childhood, our type of attachment will end up somewhere on a sliding scale of security (Figure 7). The greater inclination we have toward one of the insecure poles, the greater the problems we will have in initiating and maintaining functioning relationships.

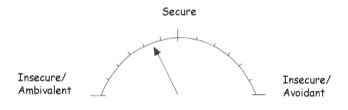

Figure 7. Our type of attachment is on a sliding scale. The secure attachment is in the middle. We will have an inclination toward either the insecure-avoidant or the insecure-ambivalent direction, depending on what our relationship model looks like.

The road to change: New experiences

There is actually nothing that prevents our relationship model from changing throughout life. Your relationship model cannot be changed, however, by thinking of new strategies for creating intimacy or by theoretically learning how relationships work. Ideas and intellectual knowledge do not take hold in the emotional memory and thus do not take hold in our relationship model either. On the other hand, what can create change is new experiences. As soon as we experience things we haven't been part of before, the emotional memory is filled with new mental images and in the long run, this may change our way of thinking, feeling and acting. Anyone who has an insecure attachment style may, for example, happen to meet an extremely secure partner who shows him or her in a practical way that intimacy can indeed persist. Such a concrete experience of a lasting love will create new images in the emotional memory and causes the relationship model to develop in a more secure direction. In that way, an insecure person can become more secure in his future relationships.

There is a catch, however, and that is that our relationship model, unfortunately, is often self-confirming. This means that it prevents us from having precisely those new experiences that would have been able to create a change. This is associated with the fact that as adults we have often come to view what the relationship model says as an obvious part of our personality. Whether we are shy or open, sensitive or repressed, happy or gloomy, we see it as something obvious and unavoidable. After all, we've been like that since we were little. This means that we often have a hard time seeing the possibilities that are beyond the limits that our own relationship model sets up.

It can be said that we are like actors playing ourselves with our inner relationship model as a script. When we've advanced a bit into adult life we hardly need to look at the script; we think we know that we function in a certain way where relationships are concerned and we think it has to be like that. In that way, we let our relationship model shape our life, instead of filling life with the kind of experiences that could change the relationship model and thus make us free to create the intimate relationships we long for.

If we want to change our way of handling relationships, we have to change our relationship model, and the only way to do that is to consciously expose ourselves to experiences that are beyond the worldview of our current relationship model. When the model tells us to create distance, then we have to get closer. When the model tells us to be suspicious, then we have to try to feel trust. When the model tells us to close up and hide what we feel, then we have to open ourselves up. This can be tricky—and for that reason we are going to devote a large part of this book to explaining how this works in practical terms.

But the reward can be great. When we expose ourselves to situations that we otherwise reflexively would have defended ourselves against, this creates a deep impression in our emotional memory. The relationship model changes and gradually what previously seemed difficult or even impossible becomes almost easy.

Later, we will talk a lot about how creating these kinds of new experiences might happen. But first we need to say something about the challenge that the need for intimacy brings to those of us who live in a modern society.

Our Ancient Longing for Intimacy

Attachment theory says that we human beings have a biological need to live close to one another. That need is seen through all of human history—from the time that we as Homo erectus left the apes behind us less than two million years ago and started developing larger brains up until we appeared as Homo sapiens two hundred thousand years ago. What made this amazing development possible was to a large degree our ancestors' capacity for creating intimacy with one another. One hundred thousand years ago, the people who lived in caves in what we now call Africa were a sociable breed. They lived from the cradle to the grave as part of a symbiotic group of perhaps forty to fifty people. They hunted and gathered food together and they helped to protect each other against a dangerous outside world. Losing contact with the group meant death. Community and intimacy were the greatest source of security and happiness in the lives of these early people.

And it's still that way today. Our societies may have changed appearance during the last hundred thousand years, but biologically and genetically, not much has changed within us. Inside us we carry the memory of two million years of community. We are not constructed for a solitary life, and involuntary solitude is therefore a torment for most of us.

But the question remains: why is loneliness spreading in first world countries? Why can many of us not fulfill our ancient need for intimacy? A conceivable explanation is that the modern possibility of surviving alone is so new that we haven't yet learned how to handle it. It's important to remember how quickly our view of solitude has changed. Even far into the twentieth century it was unusual for adults to live alone. Someone who lived alone was perceived as deviant and strange, and to ensure a secure old age it was necessary for most people to have children. Women and men (until quite recently homosexuals could not live together openly) were dependent on one another economically and socially. For two million years, from the childhood of humanity until quite recently, people have thus been forced to enter into long-term relationships based on external circumstances. As part of the bargain, so to speak, they found intimacy there.

But during our and our parents' lifetimes, society has rapidly become more and more advanced. The safety net for the individual that had always been the point of building societies has become more and more effective, and today surviving as a single person works out just fine. At the same, time social conventions and gender roles have changed so that without risk of persecution we can live a life without a partner, or we can let many short relationships follow one another and in between them live alone.

The advantage of the new freedom is naturally that we ourselves can choose which relationships we want to be in. The downside is that we can more easily reject intimacy if we associate it with too many painful emotions. Along with the fact that we live in a time where it is physically and socially possible to live alone, it is also now possible to avoid the pain of love.

This is particularly tempting for all of us who have insecure attachment patterns with us from childhood. After all, we associate love with more pain than others do. By more or less unconsciously avoiding close, lasting relationships, we can avoid pain. We experience this in the short term as a gain. But in the long term the price can be very high. Deep inside we still need love, and even if we train ourselves not to feel it, a longing for intimacy remains inside us. When we make ourselves alone, we deny ourselves one of life's most fundamental needs. And over time, this doesn't make us feel good.

The conclusion is that we are among the first people in history who have to learn to create intimate relationships out of free will—not because we won't survive otherwise, but simply because we need intimacy in order to feel good. If insecure attachments in childhood and poorly functioning relationship models stand in the way, then we have to solve those problems.

Chapter 4:

ATTACHMENT IN PRACTICE

In the first chapter we told about seven individuals, all of whom had various types of problems with creating lasting relationships. We will now return to four of them and investigate in more detail what was going on when they acquired their insecure attachment styles and how their early lives affect them as adults.

But before we do this, you're going to meet a woman whose name is Emma and who has a markedly secure attachment style. Her story will give you something to compare to when you read the stories of the insecure individuals.

Emma is secure

Emma has had a secure attachment style ever since childhood. She grew up with parents who had plenty of both time and desire to devote to her. When she cried, they were good at deciding what was causing the crying and could quickly step in with the right actions, whether Emma needed food, a dry diaper or simply the secure feeling of being close to them. Emma's parents put their daughter's needs ahead of their own. If she wanted to be hugged or carried, they almost always did so, even if they were busy with something else. And when Emma played on her own, they showed consideration by not interrupting her play, even if right at that moment they might have wanted to hug their daughter. This meant that Emma sensed that her parents accepted her and her needs. Sometimes they were tired, of course, and in a bad mood, but she still knew that they were there for her when she really needed them.

During her entire childhood, Emma was treated as a person worth loving. She did not need to act in any special way to win her parents' love, because they thought she was just fine the way she was. This shaped Emma's inner relationship model.

Emma as an adult

When Emma got older and fell in love, her relationship model gave her a solid belief that secure, loving relationships are possible. This helped her to make just those kinds of relationships a reality. As an adult Emma has a good ability to get close to and rely on other people, and this tends to bring out the best in many of those she encounters. She also has a rather easy time recognizing loving individuals when she meets them—after all, she grew up with two such people and knows how good it feels to be in their company.

When Emma meets a potential partner on a date, for example, it's pretty easy for her to be herself. Her relationship model tells her that she doesn't need to pretend in order to be loved. She manages both to listen to the other person and talk about herself. The chances are high that the date therefore feels both inspiring and secure for the potential partner.

Emma associates relationships primarily with security and intimacy, and has no particular fear of being abandoned. This means that she is able to leave her partner alone when that's required, but she can also give a lot of intimacy. When she herself needs consolation, intimacy or perhaps wants to be left alone, it is fairly easy for her to openly show that.

Emma's view of close relationships demonstrates that she does not find it necessary to control either her own behavior or her partner's behavior. Love develops at its own pace, and she relies on the fact that, in general, it tends to persist.

This does not mean that Emma, or anyone else for that matter, is free from relationship or love problems. Falling in love and trying to form a relationship with another person is a process that includes everything from the greatest happiness we can feel to the most severe pain and sorrow. No one can be certain about not being left or disappointed, and even relationships that work well go through crises. The painful feelings that are then provoked are part of life and this applies to all people, including Emma.

Let's say that someone with whom Emma is very much in love breaks up with her in an insensitive way. Then she is as sad and wounded as anyone else in this kind of situation. But Emma's secure attachment style means that she is uncommonly well-equipped to manage the disappointment. She is not going to let sorrow over the relationship that ended lead to her disparaging herself, and she is going to have a relatively easy time seeking help and support among friends or others who are close to her.

For Emma it is not a complete catastrophe to be alone either. She does pretty well in her own company, and when she's tired of it, her relationship model says there is plenty of love out there. A painful experience such as being abandoned is, according to her inner relationship model, not the rule but an exception. This is a great consolation for Emma when she finds herself in difficult situations.

Emma's positive expectations about close relationships will most likely have a certain self-confirming effect in her life. Even if not everyone she meets lives up to her expectations, the chances are great that her combined experiences in the long term will agree pretty well with what her relationship model says. When she gets old she is probably going to be able to say that most people really could be relied on, and that most responded to her wish for intimacy. Emma's secure attachment thus shapes her life in a positive way.

Matthew avoids intimacy

Now we'll meet a man named Matthew who does not have an equally easy time getting relationships to work as Emma. We talked about him briefly in the first chapter: he's the social thirty-year-old who usually has a good time on the first few dates but then always finds fault with his partner and finally pulls out of the relationship before it's had time to start.

Matthew has an insecure-avoidant attachment style. We will try to get to know Matthew a little better and see why he has this type of attachment style and what that means for him as an adult.

Matthew grew up with two stressed, hard-working parents who had a hard time living up to his demands for intimacy. When Matthew cried, his parents often let him cry without picking him up. If he reacted with despair they got angry and forced him to be alone until he calmed down. If they thought Matthew was really troublesome, they might even punish and openly reject him. Maybe they thought this would teach their son to be independent. Only if Matthew was calm and did not demand any intimacy would his parents let him be close to them every now and then. Matthew enjoyed such occasions.

For a small child, solitude is the most frightening thing there is. In order to be able to develop properly, Matthew needed access to his parents as a secure base, and like all children he had an innate ability to adapt to the parents he happened to have. Matthew used this adaptation capacity during his first few years of life to tone down his own demands for intimacy, step by step. This did not mean that his need to be carried and consoled lessened, but by noticing that such demands did not lead to more intimacy but instead to less, he learned to conceal his needs. Before he had turned two he was an expert at self-control. In this way little Matthew maximized the likelihood that his parents, despite everything, would have the energy to be with him sometimes.

The result of this process was that outwardly Matthew seemed to be an uncommonly calm, collected child. At the age of one and a half he seemed to like playing alone in a precocious way and he seldom showed his discontent about the fact that his parents had so little time left over for him.

Let's say that at age one Matthew was tested in the psychological test called the Strange Situation, as described above. When the parent gets up and leaves the room, Matthew does not change expression, even though he is now being left alone in a completely strange environment. Inside he is beside himself with worry, but he does not let on. According to his past experience with his parents, they would only push him away if he revealed his feelings.

When after a few minutes the parent comes back into the room, Matthew is just as unmoved. Perhaps he even turns his back and continues playing as if nothing had happened. This is, according to Matthew's inner relationship model, the most appropriate way to get intimacy from his parents.

It is important to understand that Matthew's inner relationship models always tried to help him get maximum intimacy from his parents. When he turns his back on them, it's not because he wants to increase the distance to his parent. Matthew turns away because his inner relationship model says that the best way to get closer is to distance himself and hope that his parents reward him with at least a little connection.

During the rest of his childhood Matthew got better and better at concealing his troublesome emotions and seeming like a happy, smart boy. When he felt sad he avoided seeking consolation from his parents. Inside himself Matthew became like two different people: outwardly a happy boy who seemed to be very independent and who appeared to get along just fine on his own—obviously his parents liked this version of Matthew. But inside himself he was a sad, angry and extremely lonely boy. His parents could not bear to catch even a glimpse of this version of Matthew, and in time Matthew himself also learned to consider this boy loathsome and impossible to love.

Matthew as an adult
The relationship model that Matthew brought with him

into adult life gives a pretty gloomy picture of "how people are." Matthew intuitively feels that people would turn away from him if they realized who he really was. For years he has tried to prevent this from happening by developing a formidable social capacity. He lives his life as a happy, social, smart and funny guy and it is easy for him to be liked at work and in other social contexts. Matthew's friends cannot understand how such a pleasant person can have problems finding someone to be with. They know nothing about Matthew's relationship model—and Matthew doesn't either. But it is a built-in advisor who constantly tells him that he has to keep an emotional distance from people around him.

When he was little Matthew learned, with the help of thoughts and conclusions, to decide how he should behave in order to be accepted by his parents. At the same time he learned to disregard his emotions. While growing up he thus received good training in reasonable thinking, but limited experience in handling his emotional life. As an adult, Matthew does not think that emotions are a particularly important part of life at all. He considers himself more the thinking type. Matthew's problem with experiencing feelings leads to him having a hard time falling in love. When he does get interested in someone, he tries to think his way forward to whether he wants a relationship or not, rather than feeling his way to that conclusion. In the relationships Matthew has been in he's been accused of being cold and distant. What no partner can understand, and what Matthew himself cannot know unless he gets some help, is that this cool distance is basically his only strategy for creating intimacy. The problem of course is that the strategy was formed to suit his parents, but doesn't work nearly as well with those he becomes interested in as an adult.

Obviously Matthew, like everyone else, has a deep longing for intimacy and he does not want to live his life alone. True, he himself does not experience this longing particularly strongly. Matthew most often formulates his wishes about life in more rational terms. He may, for example, think that it would be boring to live alone, or worry about missing the experience of being a dad. But concealed behind these reasonable thoughts is a longing for intimacy and attachment that he has missed his entire life.

Let's say that one day Matthew gets interested in someone he met through the Internet or perhaps at work. They decide to go out and have dinner. In contrast to secure Emma, Matthew can't assume that the partner will like him the way he is. Because his relationship model says that other people are basically unsympathetic, he has to try to capture their interest by showing off. He is careful about looking good and he willingly talks about his successes in his career and other things that might seem impressive. On the other hand, he does not care to talk about feelings. This does not prevent Matthew from being extremely pleasant and easy to socialize with. The strategy for creating intimacy that is stored in his inner relationship model says that he has to adapt to the needs of others in order not to be rejected and he is therefore strikingly flexible, accommodating and fun. He knows what to do to get people to feel good.

Matthew meets his potential partner a few times. Their encounters are fun and exciting, and he understands that his feelings are reciprocated. But on the third date something happens: inside Matthew the strong yearning for intimacy that has been well concealed inside him his entire life now awakens. He is not aware of it himself, but deep inside he only wants to throw himself in the arms of the woman sitting across from him and remain there.

At the same moment that these feelings show up, Matthew's relationship model reacts instantly. Thousands of snapshots of painful rejections long ago tell Matthew that he is a despicable person whom no one can love. At the same moment Matthew feels he has to increase distance.

Matthew is not conscious of what is going on inside him. The only thing he notices is that he suddenly sees faults and deficiencies in his date that he hadn't seen before. Perhaps she has the wrong interests or the wrong clothes. He thinks things have probably been moving a little fast and is struck by the fact that he really doesn't know his potential partner at all. Matthew is filled with doubt that he's even interested in her.

As we've seen before, our inner relationship models develop so that we as small children can get as close to our parents as possible. In children the relationship model played its biggest role in situations where we were most afraid of being abandoned. One such situation is evoked, for example, when the child is tested in the Strange Situation. When the parent disappears through the door, the child's inner relationship model is activated instantly and reminds him about how he ought to behave to minimize the risk of being cast out into life-long solitude. When we've become adults, the relationship model is also most active in situations when we experience that there is a risk of losing the intimacy we long for. That is why Matthew's relationship model starts making a fuss inside him only on the third date: at this point he has managed to build a certain intimacy. Now he has something to lose.

Matthew is torn between two conflicting impulses. His feelings say—even if he scarcely notices it himself—that he wants to get close. But his relationship model repeats what it has always said when he's had intimacy within reach: "Your longing must not be seen outwardly, because it will lead to you being rejected. Increase distance!"

All the brooding and doubt about the partner's suitability that suddenly arises in Matthew has only one purpose: to allow him to increase distance. It is as if the relationship model is guiding Matthew by remote control from a part of his inner self that he cannot consciously survey. In his conscious self, Matthew is convinced that all these objections are completely reasonable. He thinks he's met the wrong person. Of course, he may be right. The problem is that Matthew can't really know that at such an early stage. The fact that he was very interested on the first two encounters also indicates that this sudden doubt originates in the relationship model's demand for increased distance rather than reasonable doubts about the partner's suitability.

Even though Matthew was interested before now, suddenly he feels suffocated and closed in. The closeness he was just enjoying now seems obtrusive. If he were asked why he wants to be alone when he just seemed to be in love, he would have no answer. He is simply convinced that he has to withdraw.

For Matthew's potential partner, his avoidance behavior is incomprehensible. One day he's extremely nice and interested. The next day he goes into reverse and doesn't want to meet, or only wants to get together after long intervals. Perhaps she draws the conclusion that Matthew is no longer interested, but in reality it's the opposite. The problem is that the more he longs for intimacy, the stronger the impulse grows to increase distance and avoid hurt.

Matthew's evasive manner risks making him lonely. But he may also be lucky and meet someone who refuses to let go of him, even though he withdraws over and over. In such a case, a relationship may gradually develop despite everything. But Matthew's insecure-avoidant attachment style also shows up once he is in relationships. He continues to carefully check his behavior so that he doesn't do something that, according to his relationship model, may frighten his partner away. The result is that he does not demonstrate much affection and he feels pressured if someone wants to get very close to him emotionally.

The relationship model becomes most vocal if the relationship is subjected to difficulties. If Matthew feels the least bit uncertain about his partner's love, the relationship model recommends to him to quickly beat a retreat, conceal his emotions and increase distance. He becomes closed and aloof just when the relationship perhaps needs increased intimacy in order to survive.

Matthew's relationship model makes him lonely, and later we will show how he can change that. But first we'll meet a few other individuals who also have problems in their relationships.

Maria wants everyone to feel good

Just like Matthew, Maria has an insecure-avoidant attachment style. You met her in the first chapter of this book. She's the one who has an easy time starting relationships, but whose relationships run out in the sand because the person she's with loses interest.

Maria grew up in a family where the mother was almost always depressed and feeling bad. Maria remembers how from an early age she consoled and helped her mother in various ways. Then she received a certain amount of appreciation, but there was not much room for her to express her own needs.

Her father was the mother's opposite. He was social and active and worked a lot. Maria did not see him often enough so that they could get close to one another. When her dad was at home he often trivialized the mother's problems. This made both the mother and Maria angry and they thought he was self-centered.

As an adult, Maria has problems with her relationships. When she's together with someone it's often wonderful at the beginning, with lots of love and intimacy. She loves to make her partner feel comfortable, and initially her boyfriends enjoy being so well taken care of. Several times she's heard that she's the perfect girlfriend, and she doesn't think this is a bad goal. Going forward, however, is usually not equally fun. In time her partner becomes more and more distant. It is as if the attraction runs out of him. Maria does everything she can to get him to feel good again, but it's as if the interest subsides the more she exerts herself. In several relationships, it was later found that the men had been unfaithful to Maria.

Maria's relationship model says that other people

in general do not want her near them if she makes demands and shows that she has needs of her own. So far Maria functions exactly like Matthew. But where Matthew's insecure-avoidant attachment shows itself by his fear of even entering into lasting relationships, Maria has found an alternative way. Coexistence with her helpless, depressed mother taught Maria that she could get a certain degree of intimacy if she did everything to satisfy her mother's needs, at the same time that she concealed her own. She became her mother's caregiver, and received some intimacy in return.

This strategy was stored in Maria's relationship model, and as an adult she therefore tries to obey her partner's slightest hint. She is not aware of any other way of approaching another person. The problem is that the constant adaptation means that Maria herself becomes invisible. In some relationships Maria's boyfriends have complained that she always has to be so perfect, which hurts her. What they were really missing, without being able to express it, is an encounter with a real person with needs of her own. Without such an encounter the relationship cannot deepen, and therefore the interest of her partners subsides over time. They get tired of never really getting to know the person they're with.

When Maria seeks help, her own theory about the cause of the problem is that she hasn't managed to find a man who is truly in love with her, but this is a misperception. In the long term, people can't stay in love with someone they can't get to know. Maria thus has reason to change her relationship model.

Lena clings tight

You met Lena in the first chapter too. She is often worried about being abandoned and in her most recent relationships has demanded guarantees that her partner will have a child with her, which contributed to the relationships coming to an end.

Lena has an insecure-ambivalent attachment style from her childhood. Lena grew up in a family where both the mother and father had substance abuse problems. This meant that they were capricious in their treatment of her. When her dad was drunk he could be fun and want to play with Lena, but when he was sober he showed no interest at all. Her mother took better care of her daughter when she was sober, but couldn't manage it when she was drunk.

Lena therefore learned during her first years of life that it was not her own needs that controlled access to security. Instead it was her parents' varying ability and desire to be close to their daughter that governed their relationship. It became impossible for Lena to predict whether her parents would be available to her or not, and they could never be a secure base in her life.

Just like Matthew and Maria, Lena needed to find a strategy to get her parents to give her as much intimacy and security as possible. For Lena, the best method proved to be showing the maximum need to be taken care of. She became a clingy, demanding child who seldom wanted to play alone. Lena's strategy was successful in the sense that she actually got to experience more contact with her parents than she would have if she'd been calm and compliant like Matthew or Maria. However, this strategy could never truly reduce her constant feeling of insecurity. She watched her parents' every move and was seldom calm even when she had them in her embrace. She was angry and disappointed at her parents, and it showed.

Let's say that as a one-year-old Lena is tested in the Strange Situation. When the parent leaves her alone she becomes frightfully unhappy and cries desperately, but when the parent comes back she does not become calm. True, she signals that she wants to be picked up, but the intimacy gives her no security. Once up in the parent's arms she wants down on the floor again. She is both sad and angry even though the parent is with her, and the reason is that she knows she can't rely on them.

Lena (and others with an insecure-ambivalent attachment style) have an inner relationship model that says it is possible that people can love her, but that the risk is always great that they will suddenly change and disappear. If that happens, there's not much, according to Lena's relationship model, that she herself can do about it.

Lena as an adult
As an adult Lena longs for a close relationship, but she is very afraid of being abandoned and tends to cling, even though she realizes this may scare off the one she loves.

Let's say that Lena meets someone she likes and goes on a date. Lena is then open, happy and energetic. During her childhood she had a lot of training in living with her emotions, and this means that as an adult she is a dynamic person with whom it's exciting to associate. She can tell sensitive, fascinating stories about herself and in that way quickly create rather close contact even the first few times she meets a new acquaintance. But sometimes she opens up a little too fast. For example, as soon as the first time she meets someone she may tell intimate details about herself, her childhood or previous relationships. This is due to the fact that she is guided by her emotions to a large extent and her reasonable thoughts don't always manage to keep up. Sometimes she regrets this openness. But for the most part she is comfortable being among people.

When dating, Lena has a few exciting encounters with her new partner. She starts to feel in love and her feelings seem to be reciprocated. It is now that her inner relationship model starts playing an active role in the process. Lena suddenly becomes nervous that this love will be taken away from her.

As long as she can be together with her partner she feels fine, but immediately after an encounter she may be overcome by a strong feeling of being worthless and abandoned. Nothing of what her partner just said about how much he likes her now matters. Lena feels in all of her soul that she is going to be abandoned. The only thing that can calm her for the moment is making contact with him to have her love acknowledged.

So Lena calls, emails and texts all day long. If at some point there is a delay before she gets an answer, she gets extremely worried. A few hours of silence drives her to the point of panic. She is then convinced that her partner has changed his mind and wants to break off the romance. If she sends a message in the evening, she may lie awake at night waiting for an answer.

Lena's friends think she is acting unbalanced and try to help her think clearly. Why would the man she's in love with want to see her at all if he's not interested? When Lena hears these kinds of reasonable viewpoints from someone she knows, she can allow herself to be convinced. Her thoughts may then temporarily take control over her emotions. In such situations she realizes that there actually isn't anything that suggests that she's in the process of being abandoned and she can decide to take it easy and not get unnecessarily stressed. But an hour later, once her friend has gone home, the panic comes back. The reasonable thoughts no longer have an effect and the strong feeling of being abandoned again takes power over Lena.

Lena's new partner has a hard time understanding her. He likes her, sees her often and would like to keep doing so. But it's as if she doesn't trust him. No matter how wonderful a time they have together, she starts doubting whether his interest is real as soon as they're apart. She calls so often that he starts to feel monitored. Lena's lack of trust means that the mood gets worse and worse in the budding relationship.

In her relationships Lena wants to get as close as possible, as quickly as possible. The period of testing and investigation that must exist at the beginning of all relationships is much too painful for her. She wants quick guarantees that she won't be left. It doesn't matter how much her partner protests his love, she still has constant catastrophic thoughts that the intimacy will disappear.

Lena is often perceived as clingy, but she can also be strongly rejecting. On one occasion she'd arranged a meeting with a man she'd made contact with over the Internet and was interesting in getting to know better. The man came ten minutes late to their first meeting, and that was enough for her to judge him as unreliable and break off contact. Sometimes clinging tightly one second and breaking off the relationship the next is typical for many who have an insecure-ambivalent attachment style.

Lena has been abandoned several times because many people simply can't put up with her. Yet she repeats the same behavior in relationship after relationship. The relationship model is thus no longer fulfilling its purpose. This prevents Lena from experiencing intimacy.

Johan can't make up his mind

Johan from the first chapter also has an insecure-ambivalent attachment style. He has a pretty easy time starting relationships, but he can't stop doubting whether he's really met the right person. This means that his relationships end after a while because his partner gets tired of never getting a clear "yes."

Johan grew up with overprotective parents. They longed for a child, but they were forced to try for many years and suffer several miscarriages before Johan arrived at last. Johan's parents were overjoyed at finally having a child and they did everything they could so their son would feel secure and happy.

By protecting Johan, his parents were actually to a large extent satisfying their own need for intimacy, tenderness and feeling needed. Johan's needs came second. True, he might often feel very loved, but his parents took care of him in a way that caused him to doubt his own ability to manage life. He became uncertain of his own value and this came to characterize his relationship model.

His image of how other people might function became complicated. On the one hand he learned that there was a possibility of being loved, but he also learned to doubt that people really cared about him. During therapy Johan confessed that when he was sick while growing up his parents might say, "We hope you're better soon so that we'll be happy again." The image that characterizes his relationship model says that people are generally considerate, but not completely reliable.

Johan as an adult
Now when Johan meets someone he likes, he feels a deep longing to get really close. But at the same time he has a hard time knowing whether the relationship satisfies his own needs or only his partner's. He often doubts whether he's met the right person. The result is that Johan enters into relationships, but he has a very hard time definitively saying yes to the partner. It's as if he is waiting for someone else to make the major decision for him, and he seems to be able to wait indefinitely. He can put off decisions such as whether he should move in together or have a child for years until his partner finally gets tired and leaves him. Then Johan becomes desperate, because he really longs for intimacy. But his relationship model stands in the way.

The Various Relationship Models

The stories of Emma, Matthew, Maria, Lena and Johan show how much significance our attachment style has for our way of handling relationships. We all have our own carefully constructed relationship model inside us, and we use it constantly to define how other people function and how we should best handle intimacy. We will now summarize what distinguishes the various types of attachment (Table 1).

	IMAGE OF OTHERS	REACTION TO CHANCE FOR INTIMACY AND STRESS	WHAT CON-TROLS YOU
Secure	People are accessible and empa-thetic	Feels trust and gets closer	Interplay of thoughts and emotions
Insecure – avoidant	People are unsympa-thetic or too intrusive	Keeps distance, sometimes via exaggerated adaption	Thoughts
Insecure – ambivalent	People are capricious and unpre-dictable	Alternately clingy and dis-tant	Emotions

Table 1. What the relationship model says about others and about the best way to create a relation-ship depends on what attachment type you have.

Individuals with secure attachment styles assume that other people in general are accessible and empathetic. When they are attracted to someone and face the possibility of creating an intimate relationship, they feel trust and therefore dare to get closer.

Individuals with an insecure-avoidant attachment style view others as either unsympathetic or annoyingly intrusive. When they are attracted to someone they react by keeping an emotional and/or physical distance. But they can also maintain the distance by trying to satisfy the partner's needs to such a degree that they themselves become invisible in the relationship.

Those who have an insecure-ambivalent attachment style see other people as capricious and difficult to rely on. When they become interested in someone they may alternate between being clingy and strongly rejecting the other person.

Are You Controlled By Thoughts or Emotions?

Our attachment type determines to what extent we are controlled by our thoughts or our emotions. You will see this distinction at the far right in the table above. Let's give a few concrete examples of how our behavior can be controlled by thoughts and/or emotions.

Matthew is governed by thoughts
Matthew has an insecure-avoidant attachment style and learned even when he was little that it did not work to reveal his own emotional needs to his parents. To avoid being rejected, he needed to conceal and overlook his emotions, and instead think his way to what he should, and shouldn't, do to satisfy his parents' needs. Naturally there were always emotions inside Matthew, but he did not get much practice in handling them. He got even more practice in thinking rationally, and therefore developed into being governed by thoughts. When Matthew decides what he is going to do and not do in

his life, those decisions are almost always the product of his thoughts, not of his emotions. As an adult Matthew has a hard time talking about feelings even with his closest friends, and if you ask him what he feels he often answers that he doesn't know.

The ability to think rationally is naturally a valuable quality. For example, Matthew is very good at organizing work in an efficient way and therefore gets more done than many others at work. In connection with relationships, however, being governed by thoughts causes problems. Matthew has a hard time falling in love and is uncertain about what he's really looking for in a possible future partner.

This is a common problem for people with insecure-avoidant attachment styles. A man who went into therapy with Egil was asked what qualities his ideal partner should have. He answered that she had to be good-looking, not too tall, have large breasts, be smart and preferably have worked as a model. All of these wishes are products of thoughts; there are no emotional needs here at all. This man naturally has emotional needs as much as anyone else, but because he is governed by thoughts and ideals, such needs have no room in his dream vision, and this makes it harder for him to find anyone he can function with.

Lena is governed by emotions

Lena has an insecure-ambivalent attachment style. When she was little she learned that her parents were far too capricious and unpredictable for her to be able to think her way to a behavior that suited them. If, on the other hand, Lena gave vent to strong emotions, she could gain her parents' attention. She cried and complained a lot, and often appeared anxious and in need of consolation. Lena therefore got a lot of practice in venting her emotions, and she therefore developed into being largely governed by emotions.

This characterizes Lena's life as an adult. She lets her emotions govern many decisions, and this makes her a creative, dynamic person who can quickly find solutions that individuals governed more by thoughts aren't able to see. In her relationships she may, thanks to this emotional governance, experience strong passions, but this also creates a number of problems. When Lena feels insecure, this too releases very strong emotions inside her. In such situations she really needs to use reasonable thoughts to counter these emotions and question whether they are wisely motivated or not. But Lena has a hard time doing this, and she therefore risks being swept along by her inner emotional storms.

Secure Emma lets thoughts and emotions interact

Emma has a secure attachment style, and in contrast to Matthew and Lena she has the ability to let thoughts and emotions interact in suitable proportions. This means that she can allow her emotions to have greater latitude when this is appropriate, and let her thoughts play a greater role when they can do a better job. This is an advantage in all situations in life, not least in relationships. Emma has contact with her emotional needs; she knows what she's looking for in a relationship and notices when something is wrong. In difficult situations—when for example, she is worried about being left—she can both experience her worry and, by thinking, make a cooler analysis of the actual situation. This gives her more alternatives for action than Matthew and Lena would have had in the same situation.

Later we will return to our thoughts and emotions and show how we can get them to interact better. But first we'll see what happens when people with different types of attachment styles meet.

When Different Attachment Styles Meet

When you meet a partner, your respective relationship models are going to influence each other. Exactly how this happens naturally depends on who you are and how you function. But certain rough patterns can be distinguished. Certain attachment types simply tend to be drawn to one another, while others don't function equally well together.

Individuals who have a secure attachment style often have a relatively easy time building relationships, regardless of what attachment type their partner has. If the one who is secure meets someone who is also secure, the result is often a stable, long-term relationship with a lot of intimacy. If the one who is secure meets someone who is insecure-avoidant or insecure-ambivalent, then the secure partner's view of relationships may infect the insecure partner, who then has a chance to become a bit more secure as well.

If two individuals who both have an insecure-avoidant attachment style were to fall in love, then it gets trickier. Both tend to keep distance from the other, and the entire relationship is dominated by thoughts rather than emotions. Such a relationship tends to be extremely reasonable, and the risk exists that dynamics and passion suffers.

The exact opposite applies if two individuals who both have an insecure-ambivalent attachment style fall in love with one another. Both parties then strive to quickly get really close to the other, and the result can be an extremely impassioned relationship. The problem is that people with an insecure-ambivalent attachment style may also push their partners away in situations where, for example, they don't feel sufficiently loved or get jealous. When both parties in a relationship act in that way, the result may be a steady alternation of dramatic breakups and emotional reunions. The relationship may be extremely stormy.

It seems to be relatively unusual, however, that people with the same type of insecure attachment style are attracted to one another. It is more common that we are drawn to individuals who can contribute the kind of rational or emotional governance that we lack ourselves. It is this mechanism that we often phrase as "opposites attract" or that certain couples "complement one another." Someone who is insecure therefore easily falls for someone who is either secure or (perhaps even more common) someone who is insecure but in a different way. In the latter case the result is a relationship where the one party has an insecure-avoidant attachment style and the other an insecure-ambivalent style. If two different types of insecure attachment styles meet, this may lead to the respective relationship models strengthening each other. This can have dynamic effects, and we will now look more closely at how this dynamic might function in a hypothetical relationship.

When avoidant Matthew meets ambivalent Lena

One day Matthew (insecure-avoidant) and Lena (insecure-ambivalent) meet one another and fall in love. The attraction is reinforced by the fact that they have different attachment patterns. Matthew sees in Lena a dynamic person who causes him to feel alive. This is naturally due to the fact that Lena, with her strong emotions, can awaken a part of Matthew's dormant emotional life. He thinks it's lovely to let himself be infected by what he experiences as Lena's desire for life.

Lena sees in Matthew a collected, intelligent person who seems to have a handle on most things. She feels that he may be someone to hold onto when emotional storms are raging inside her. (If you think Matthew and Lena resemble gender stereotypes too strongly, then just exchange their genders. There are many women who have an insecure-avoidant attachment style and men who have an insecure-ambivalent attachment style.)

Matthew and Lena feel that they suit each other like two puzzle pieces. Passion blossoms. But after two or three amazing encounters, something happens. When Matthew is alone after the date he starts wondering who Lena really is and whether she really is right for him. He thinks that perhaps the relationship is developing a little too fast. And then he decides to put his foot on the brake so that he has time to think about whether Lena really is a good match.

What has happened is that Matthew's relationship model has been activated. It says that he now finds himself much too close to another person and that he has to increase distance so as not to risk being rejected. He therefore makes himself unavailable for a few days. This comes as a shock to Lena. She has gotten to be just as close as she wants to be, but suddenly this intimacy is pulled away from her. This causes her relationship model to also be activated. Lena feels a sense of desperation growing within her. She does everything to make contact with Matthew and demands to see him. She is now controlled almost entirely by her painful emotions and cannot bide her time alone, even for a few days.

Lena's attempts to get close cause Matthew to feel even more pressured and reinforce his need to distance himself. When Lena calls he doesn't answer his phone, or else he answers and says vaguely and unsympathetically that he has a lot to do but they maybe they can see each other in a week or so. Lena is beside herself with worry. She is convinced that Matthew has gotten tired of her and she can't sleep at night. After a few days she is so agitated that she starts pushing Matthew away from her. She stops trying to call, but still thinks uninterruptedly about Matthew and feels awful about what is happening.

If Lena stays away long enough, the probability is great that Matthew will again approach her. This could be called the rubber-band effect, and implies that the urge for intimacy increases with distance. Matthew does long deep inside for intimacy, and when he perceives that a relationship is about to end this may provoke worry that allows him to come closer again. Matthew and Lena will likely end up in each other's arms and suddenly it will be as if their worries have been swept away. But as soon as they're apart, their relationship models come to the forefront again. Matthew gets cold feet because he is once again realizing that he has gotten too close. Lena again feels worthless and needs confirmation that she hasn't been forgotten. And so begins a new round.

There is a risk that what started as attraction is soon a ruined relationship where Matthew and Lena view one another with distrust and disappointment. Both have had their respective image of relationships stored in their respective relationship models confirmed. It has been confirmed for Lena that she can't rely on people because they disappear. It has been confirmed for Matthew that intimacy doesn't work. What they do not understand is that the relationship models are self-fulfilling. They themselves have created the situations they are suffering from.

If Matthew and Lena learn to go against what their relationship models say in certain cases, they have a greater chance of successfully creating a sustainable relationship.

We will devote the rest of this book to talking about how to set relationship models aside and do the kind of thing that might have seemed impossible before. But first we want to say a few words about how the various attachment types are valued in the culture in which we live.

Our Fear of Intimacy

A man who is in therapy with Egil tells him one day, beaming with happiness, that he has met a woman and that he is deeply in love. She works at the same place he does, but in a different department. He thinks this is fortunate: "Otherwise it wouldn't have worked."

Egil asks the client why he thinks it's good that he

only gets to see this woman on evenings and weekends. If they love one another, shouldn't they want to see each other during the day too?

"No," the man answers, "that wouldn't be good."

Egil never gets an answer as to why it wouldn't be good. The man simply assumes that the relationship will be damaged if he spends too many hours of the day with his beloved.

He is far from alone in believing this. In our culture there is a great deal of consensus that relationships benefit when intimacy is rationed. We say that relationships lose excitement if we see our partner too often. But however widespread this idea is, it's deeply wrong. It is true that many people today have problems getting their relationships to continue. But this is due in general not to the fact that people associate too much with the one they're with, but rather that they hardly manage to see each other at all. The idea that relationships should benefit from distance is like believing in trolls and gnomes. You might ask why the idea is so widespread.

A possible explanation is that the society in which we live suffers from a kind of collective variation of the insecure-avoidant attachment style. Behaviors that are actually part of this attachment type have been raised to ideals instead of being seen as problematic. Everywhere we see how people's fundamental need for intimacy is dismissed as a weakness rather than as a valuable, necessary asset. In films, TV and advertising we are fed images of people who do not need anyone other than themselves and who for that very reason are successful and happy.

When we are teenagers and it's time to initiate our

own love relationships, we learn not to be too eager. When we're standing in a bar, hoping to meet someone we will like, we often try to look indifferent. No longing for intimacy is allowed to shine through. If despite everything we do meet someone we like, we've learned that plenty of time should pass before we contact that person again, otherwise we'll reveal that we're "too" interested.

Society's unwillingness to say yes to intimacy obviously extends into many relationships. It's not unusual that couples are almost afraid to do things as a couple. When it's time to go on vacation, for example, friends have to go along. What could have been an intimate co-existence with lots of closeness and deepened contact then turns into a school trip.

In reality, our culture's fear of intimacy is based on a misunderstanding of what freedom and independence are. It is true that an independent person can manage to act on his or her own when such is required, and that this is a valuable characteristic. But the prerequisite for such independence to arise is that we must first be able to create the intimacy we need. Someone who does not dare expose himself to intimacy may pretend to be free and independent, but no genuine experience of freedom will come about. The gnawing longing for intimacy will always darken the life experience. There is only one way to genuine independence and freedom, and that goes by way of intimacy with other people.

All of us are influenced by living in a society that considers intimacy a dangerous thing. Those who have a secure attachment style from childhood also get signals from all directions about the value of distance. The risk is therefore that a person like secure Emma learns as a teenager to act with more avoidance than what really feels natural to her. This is a shame, because intimacy between people is not a problem, but a solution.

Chapter 5:

FROM INITIAL ATTRACTION TO A LASTING RELATIONSHIP

In the first chapter we talked about the relationship staircase. We have to make our way up this staircase if we're going to create a lasting, close relationship. But there is a risk that our relationship model will cause us to stumble on the stairs. Exactly how this happens depends on our particular relationship model and at what point we find ourselves on the staircase. The strength of the relationship model's influence differs on the various steps.

When we are completely alone, the relationship model is basically switched off—there is no intimacy to defend. As singles we may have rich associations with our friends, but that doesn't mean the relationship model needs to be activated. In such contexts we seldom run any risk of losing out on intimacy. This explains why we often feel relatively relaxed and content with ourselves, as long as we're alone or together with close friends. But that feeling of balance can disappear in a moment when we meet an unfamiliar person who could be a potential partner. What happens then is that the relationship model is activated inside us. This effect is often easy to see in other people. Everyone has probably seen how a friend, who has been relaxed and at ease with himself all evening, suddenly freezes up when an unfamiliar person of the appropriate gender shows up. That's how it can look when the relationship model is plugged in.

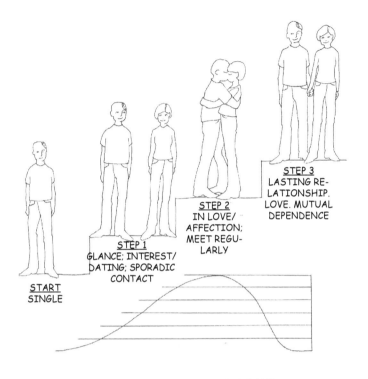

INFLUENCE OF THE RELATIONSHIP MODEL

Figure 8. The influence of the relationship model. The more intimacy you subject yourself to, the more you are influenced by your inner relationship model. It is already activated on the first step and often plays an increasingly stronger role on Step Two. On Step Three, however, the relationship model falls silent. We are by then so secure in the relationship that we no longer need to be afraid of losing it.

Some single people think that if they simply train themselves regularly in being alone, then their cultivated calm will still remain when one day they meet someone they want to be with. This strategy doesn't work, however. However secure and content with ourselves we may be in isolation, the situation is going to seem completely different when the relationship model kicks into action. Thus the only way to change your way of handling relationships is to meet new people and thus let the relationship model be activated.

The relationship model is thus activated on the first staircase step, but for many people it has an even more important part to play on the second step. This is because by that point we have become closer to our partner and have more intimacy to lose if the relationship were to end. When we reach the third step, however, the relationship model's significance is reduced. At that point we have created a lasting relationship and can relax. But when we are again subjected to stress or the relationship enters a crisis, then the relationship model starts functioning again (Figure 8).

Problems in Relationships

What the problems we may have in relationships look like depends on what our relationship model looks like. To illustrate this we will see how our seven case individuals handle the relationship staircase.

Gustav only gets to the first step
Gustav is a man who has lots of brief contacts, often

one-night stands, but who goes home before daybreak. He is one of those who isn't able to stay on the first staircase step long enough for a relationship to start.

Gustav has an insecure-avoidant attachment style from his childhood. His parents were successful businesspeople who invested heavily in professional careers while Gustav was taken care of by a series of nannies. The parents could not cope with Gustav demanding anything from them, and consistently rejected his desire for intimacy and protection.

As an adult Gustav is an apparently carefree, smart and socially gifted man who easily arouses the interest of women. Through his many brief connections he satisfies his longing for intimacy to some degree, but according to his relationship model the intimacy most often becomes dangerously great as soon as the morning after such an encounter. He then gets restless and wants to be by himself. The worry is so strong that sometimes Gustav has to go home already during the night. Once he's out on the sidewalk he may feel a deep sense of relief. A day or two later, however, he may be dejected by the thought of how far away he is from the lasting relationship he actually dreams of.

If we look at the relationship staircase we see that Gustav's relationship model already reacts when he gets up on the first step. He can handle short visits there, but quickly returns to the secure solitude at the foot of the stairs. In this way, Gustav lives his life constantly hopping back and forth between the starting point and the first step as he meets and leaves new acquaintances.

Lena wants to take the elevator to the third step

Another one who has problems with the first step is Lena. She's the thirty-four-year-old who prefers having passionate relationships, is worried about being abandoned, who sometimes is clingy and demands guarantees that the one she's with will want to have a child with her.

Lena has an insecure-ambivalent attachment style, which means that she doesn't really succeed in the initial test period that starts on the first step and continues onto the second. If we look at the relationship staircase, we see that Lena is trying to get out of passing the first and second step, and instead wants to take an elevator directly to the security of Step Three. Uncertainty feels like torture to her and she demands guarantees that the love is genuine before it has even had a chance to develop. This has scared away men who perhaps would have been very interested in being with her if she had given them more time. The only thing Lena notices is that time and time again she slides back to the starting point.

Marcus hesitates before the first step

Marcus also has problems with the first step. He's the one who often goes home if someone new shows interest in him. In order to avoid the feeling of failure, he refuses to go to parties and events where there are people he doesn't know.

Marcus has an insecure-avoidant attachment style and lives with a feeling of not being good enough. He has several siblings and grew up in a family where it was important to succeed. His parents were respected

academics and his siblings also came to be high achiev-
ers both at school and in their careers. In his family you
never talked about how you were feeling, only about
what you had achieved and how much you earned. To
be successful as a person was synonymous with having
a good career.

Like his siblings, Marcus went to a fine school and
had no problems with his studies. But he never really
attained the level of his siblings. When Marcus meets
a woman who shows interest in him, his relationship
model says that she is going to reject him if he doesn't
manage to live up to a number of unstated require-
ments. Marcus doesn't believe he can fulfill these re-
quirements and is filled with feelings of shame at how
unsuccessful he is. He isn't able to see that those around
him do not perceive him that way. The greater the interest and appreciation he encounters from others, the
stronger his performance anxiety becomes.

Marcus seldom manages to make his way to the first
step on the relationship staircase. If he encounters the
slightest interest, the relationship model forces him to
jump back down to the starting point.

Matthew stumbles on the second step

Matthew is the social, intelligent thirty-year-old who
after a few initial dates usually finds such serious faults
in the one he's met that the relationship has to be bro-
ken off.

Matthew has an insecure-avoidant attachment style.
He has a hard time showing people who he really is,
and has a much easier time showing an attractive fa-
cade. Matthew therefore feels pretty secure on the first

step when he meets a new partner the first few times. Then there are no serious demands for intimacy, and he is free to show a superficial, idealized image of himself.

After a few dates, however, he and his partner have started to get to know each other a little. The interest seems to be mutual and it would be natural to start seeing one another more regularly, which means a stride up to the second step. But now Matthew has problems because his relationship model prevents him from openly showing that he needs someone. He is filled with critical thoughts about the partner's value and starts doubting his own desire to have a relationship. This means that the relationship can't get a foothold on the second step. Matthew seems to prefer staying on the first step and maintaining the rather loose ties to the partner that are more natural there.

If he hasn't happened to find an extremely understanding, secure partner, the risk is great that his avoidant behavior destroys his growing relationship and sends him back to the solitude at the foot of the stairs.

Johan gets stuck on the second step

Another one who has problems with the second step is Johan, whom you first met in Chapter One. He is the thirty-five-year-old who has had quite a few relationships but who constantly doubts whether he should really stay in them.

Johan has an insecure-ambivalent attachment style and his relationship model prevents him from relying on his partner. He manages the first staircase step fine and makes his way rather easily to the second. But for him the trial period never ends. He may remain in the relationship a long time, but sways ambivalently back and forth between the impulse to stay and the impulse to get out. Johan's fear of definitively saying yes means that the relationship gets stuck on the second step and finally his partner gets tired of it.

Beatrice also gets stuck on the second step

Beatrice falls in love with married men and may have long relationships as a mistress, but can't get interested in someone who's available.

Beatrice has an insecure-ambivalent attachment style and therefore cannot trust that someone will stay with her in the long term. By becoming a mistress to an occupied man, she creates a relationship that may be relatively lasting but won't trigger her fear of being betrayed. Because the man already has a relationship, Beatrice is essentially rejected from the start and therefore risks no unpleasant surprises. In this way, Beatrice makes her way to Step Two in her capacity as a mistress, and she may remain there for years.

The problem is that Beatrice feels diminished by the arrangement. She has made attempts to create relationships with men who are available. But with those she barely makes it to the first step, because her opinion has been that every single one of them was unendurably boring. This too is obviously an expression of Beatrice's strong fear of being rejected. Her relationship model decides that only unavailable men may be interesting because in their company she avoids her worry of being abandoned to a certain degree.

Sometimes Beatrice has demanded that her lover leave his relationship and devote himself entirely to

Beatrice. If this were to become a reality though, the risk is great that Beatrice herself would end the relationship. Her relationship model would then warn her of the risk of being abandoned, which would force her to make her way back to the secure solitude at the foot of the staircase.

Maria only pretends to leave the first step

Maria is the woman who has such a great need to adapt herself to her partners that she herself becomes invisible and her relationships run out in the sand. Maria has an insecure-avoidant attachment style from childhood and therefore she feels very comfortable on the first step. There she is not expected to give very much of herself, and can excel in getting her partner to feel good.

After a while Maria's partner wants to make the move up to the next step and start meeting regularly. Maria has nothing against this and everything seems to be peaceful and harmonious. But even though the relationship has now entered a more intimate phase, Maria continues to act as if she were on a date with a stranger. She persists in playing the perfect girlfriend and adapts herself entirely to her partner's needs. In this way she makes herself invisible to her partner and does not risk getting too close.

After a few months or perhaps even a few years, the partner realizes that he doesn't know Maria much better than he did when they were dating. The relationship ends and Maria is alone again. The risk is that she thinks that the relationship ended because the boyfriend was not entirely satisfied with her, and so in her

next relationship she will go even further with the behaviors that lead to her being alone.

The Key Word Is "Control"

As you see, the problems on the relationship staircase
may appear quite different, depending on who we are
and what our relationship model looks like. If you analyze the various difficulties a little more closely, however, a pattern emerges. The relationship model always
forces us at one point or another to take control over a
situation that we think may lead to painful rejection.
What this control looks like will vary. If you have an
insecure-avoidant attachment style, you primarily
practice self-control. Perhaps you distance yourself or
adapt to your partner's needs so much that he or she
can't get to know you. If, on the other hand, you have
an insecure-ambivalent attachment style, you may try
to control your partner. Perhaps you try to hold on tight
to him or her, demand an unreasonable amount of confirmation or want various types of guarantees that he
or she loves you. Regardless of which control method
is used, the risk is always that this will lead to us stum-
bling or getting stuck somewhere on the staircase. If we
want to be able to create a close, lasting relationship,
we have to do something about our way of exercising
control.

Everyone needs control

Let's first figure out what control means. Imagine that
you're out skiing in the mountains. You notice it's

starting to get windy. It only takes a weak wind for your mind to start creating an image of you in a violent snowstorm. In turn this inner image releases emotions—you now fear freezing to death. Even though the weather is still beautiful, you are creating inside yourself an emotional sample of how it would have felt to find yourself in a life-threatening situation. You become, so to speak, afraid in advance. This fear motivates you to take control over a situation that is not yet dangerous, but that risks becoming dangerous if not controlled. So you act. You turn around and look for shelter, long before the storm is actually upon you.

Constructing images of a theoretical future by means of thoughts and thereby unleashing samples of the emotions that this future could hold is a valuable quality that helps us survive in all possible contexts. For example, in contrast to most other animals, we look around before we cross a road. We build warm houses in summer and are thus prepared when winter comes. And we build advanced societies where we help organize healthcare, legal systems and other safety nets so that we all avoid living in fear of future accidents. Major portions of human culture are the result of our unique capacity to create images of more or less threatening future scenarios, to allow the images to unleash emotions and then to control our behavior so that the future will be as emotionally pleasing as possible. This capacity for control is an asset, not a problem.

The first threat we learn to control is the threat of being left alone when we are small. If our parents didn't succeed in giving us as much intimacy as we needed, we developed methods for controlling the relationship. We acted like the wise skier. By studying our parents' behavior we could discover threats of rejection and loneliness well in advance. And then we acted to eliminate the threat, either by controlling our own behavior or by attempting to control our parents, depending on our attachment style. As long as we were small, this control system was necessary and useful, because it helped us maximize the vital closeness to our parents. But this does not mean that all types of control are equally advantageous.

When control becomes a problem

The problem is that our way of controlling our relationship with our parents when we're little is stored in our relationship models. When we become adults we continue to use the same old methods. When we have intimacy within reach, our relationship model creates an image inside us of how we'll be rejected. This image generates a foretaste of the emotions we think a rejection will unleash, and this foretaste awakens a strong need in us to take control over what we now see as a dangerous situation. The result is that we distance ourselves or cling too tight, depending on what our relationship model looks like.

Let's say that Matthew, who has an insecure-avoidant attachment style, has become interested in a woman and sees her a few times. Because Matthew's inner relationship model is insecure, a foretaste is created inside him of the emotions he learned a long time ago that rejection entails. He feels sad and ashamed. Matthew knows instinctively that he can get rid of such unpleasant potential emotions if he applies the type of self-control his relationship model prescribes. He can, for example, create distance to the same woman that he was recently very interested in.

Let's now say that Matthew had refrained from controlling the situation and instead continued to see his partner. In that case, the relationship would have continued to develop, though the emotional foretaste of rejection would likely remain inside Matthew. He would have felt like a skier who notices that the wind is starting to pick up on the mountain, but who instead of seeking shelter skis on right into the storm. It might feel dangerous and wrong not to retreat. But it is important to understand that in reality there is no storm. The risk scenario that our relationship models construct are based on childhood experiences and in reality can't be applied to our adult relationships at all. By using our old control methods, we are not warding off a real risk of being rejected and alone. All we are warding off are the emotions that the idea of a possible future failure arouses in us. These emotions are really quite harmless. But when we use control to avoid experiencing emotions, we create a genuine threat: the risk of being alone.

There are many ways to take control of ourselves or our potential partners in order to avoid experiencing troublesome emotions. Here are a few examples.

- Only meet new partners, have sex with them and then break off the relationship.
- Avoid socializing with a new date unless all your friends are along too. In this way, the potential partner is reduced to "one of the gang" and any genuine intimacy becomes difficult to develop.
- Act indifferent.
- Try to control the partner's every move.
- Limit yourself to brief relationships, and break them off when coexistence starts feeling boring

(which sometimes means that genuine intimacy is about to arise, which causes the relationship model to start making a fuss).

- Enter into relationships when you're traveling abroad, but not when you're at home. This is a sure way to avoid the risk of being rejected, because the relationship ends when the vacation does.
- Be the lover/mistress of occupied partners.
- Constantly wonder whether the one you're with is the "right" one. This blocks the possibility of intimacy.
- Continue looking for new contacts via the Internet even though you've already started a relationship—a good way to prevent existing relationships from deepening.
- Live separately. This may be a way to permanently remain on the second staircase step and never need to say yes to one another.
- Dream that "the right one" will show up and reject everyone who actually shows up. (We will return to the dream of "the right one" later).
- Place unreasonable demands on the partner and break off the relationship when he or she can't live up to them.

Avoidance — the ultimate control method

The more we try to avoid experiencing unwanted emotions, the more control we have to use when we try to form relationships. It is impossible to initiate a relationship without occasionally feeling fear, sorrow or other emotions that have a negative charge for most of us. The purpose of avoiding the experience of negative emotions transforms what could have been an exciting, developing love adventure to a dogged struggle where the control systems are constantly revved up. Trying to get to know new people under such circumstances can be so exhausting that many people at last resort to the most effective control method there is: avoidance.

Avoidance entails that we simply keep as far away from possible relationships as possible. We only socialize with people we already know well. We avoid situations where we might get interested in a potential partner. If a stranger were to show interest in us, we would reflexively reject him or her. We adapt ourselves to the single life and perhaps try to replace the lack of intimacy with intense association with friends. Perhaps we try to train ourselves to "enjoy our own company." Life is put in a waiting position. Perhaps we pin our hopes on one day meeting someone who is "right" and who can miraculously give us a relationship that doesn't involve any troublesome emotions.

Avoidance is an effective way to avoid experiencing pain. But the gain is short-term, because avoidance makes it impossible for us to change our relationship models, and this means that in the long term we become even more alone.

It's not possible to stop controlling

You might think that the solution is simply to "release control," and this is what many self-help books maintain. Unfortunately this is not serious advice, because it's completely impossible to release control over our lives more than on isolated occasions. In our culture these occasions usually arise when we drink alcohol, because alcohol reduces our fear and thereby also our need for control. In a sufficiently intoxicated condition, we may be ready to go all the way to the third step of the relationship staircase on the first date. Things don't appear equally simple the next day, however, when the alcohol has left the bloodstream and the relationship model has awakened. Perhaps, like Gustav, we can't even bear to be with our new acquaintance past breakfast.

In reality, our way of acting in an intoxicated condition shows how strong our capacity for control is. When we're drunk we dare to do fun things such as talk with strangers, but drunken people may also get the idea of balancing on balcony railings or exposing themselves and others to mortal danger by driving drunk. We should be happy that in a sober condition we don't think such ideas are particularly good.

Control is thus a protective mechanism that neither can nor ought to be switched off. On the other hand, what we can do is to take control of the control. This means that we can learn to use our capacity for control in such a way that it increases the possibilities for intimacy. In the remaining four chapters of this book we will talk about how this happens.

Chapter 6:
YOUR ACTIONS

Whatever you do in life, whether it's simply making coffee or something as complex as entering into a love relationship, the activity requires that three systems co-operate. These systems are your actions, your thoughts and your emotions (Figure 9).

These three systems influence each other. What you do affects what you think and feel. What you think and feel affects what you do, and at the same time your thoughts and emotions influence each other. The three systems work so closely together that they can be described as interwoven. Everyone has their own way of weaving together actions, thoughts and emotions. There are just as many variations on this interplay as there are fingerprints. You might say that your entire personality is determined by how these three systems interact in your particular life.

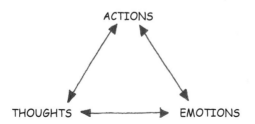

Figure 9. Your actions, your emotions and your thoughts influence each other. In combination, these three systems guide everything you do in life.

If we have problems with building relationships, this is due to the fact that our inner relationship model influences the interplay between actions, thoughts and emotions in a negative way. An important purpose of the interplay in such cases is to control our life so that we avoid experiencing unwanted emotions. In that case we need to fine-tune the three systems so they can cooperate better and lead us closer to the goals we have in life.

In the rest of this chapter we will concentrate on how one of the systems—our actions—can be fine-tuned. In later chapters we will discuss thoughts and emotions.

Your actions set the course for your life

Ultimately it is your actions that decide how your life takes shape. It's true that you can explain actions by investigating the thoughts and emotions that affect the action. But however much we dig into our past and figure out causes for why things are the way they are, it can't be escaped that our past is a bygone chapter. What forms how the rest of our lives will look is what we do right now.

We act uninterruptedly during our waking hours. Some actions change our lives dramatically. Perhaps we quit a job, have a child or move to another country. It's easy to see that such actions are significant, but we also carry out innumerable and apparently insignificant actions that can be at least equally decisive. When, for example, you go out and meet a friend for coffee, you also change the starting point for the rest of your life.

While walking to the coffee shop, while having coffee and on the way home, many things can happen that create alternatives for action that previously did not exist. The future effects can be enormous. Say that your grandfather, late one evening when he was in his twenties, decided to stop by the amusement park before he went home for the night, and that this led to his meeting your grandmother. In such a case, this simple impulse led not only to the start of a relationship, but to an entire family tree, including you, being created out of nothing. Most of what happens in our lives is in this way the result of actions that seemed completely trivial at the moment they happened. We can call this chance. But if we want to create the kind of life that we truly want, we need to help put chance on the right track.

Actions that create problems

If you look more closely at the problems people have, you discover that they are often caused by one or more actions that lead us away from the life we really want to live, but which we still tend to repeat time after time without feeling that we can do anything about it. Therefore, changing our lives entails changing our actions. There is no other way to change.

This is not as obvious as it may sound. For much of the twentieth century, psychotherapy was dominated by the so-called psychodynamic school. This approach is focused on changing emotions rather than changing actions. It was believed that one could get undesired behaviors in adult life to disappear if, with the help of several years of psychoanalysis, difficult experiences from childhood that were behind the problems were processed and recognized.

However, it has proven that our actions have a capacity to live a life of their own. As adults we are accustomed to weaving together actions, thoughts and emotions in a certain way. We have lived with our relationship model for many years now, and we identify with it. The force of habit is so great that our way of acting, thinking and feeling has in practice been disconnected from its origin and become synonymous with who we think we are.

This means that behavior will not necessarily change, even if after many years of psychoanalysis we were to succeed in finding the points in childhood when our emotional pain arose. Often, after long periods of analysis, we discover that life goes on more or less as before.

During the past twenty years another branch of psychotherapy, cognitive psychotherapy, has gained importance. This branch considers it more effective to directly attempt to influence the behaviors that do not work. This does not rule out a simultaneous interest in the origin of the problems. For example, by reading a book like this you can learn what attachment theory says about how relationship problems arise and wonder about what traces your own childhood has left behind. But cognitive psychology does not assume that understanding the origin of the problem can create change. For this it is required that we actively work on the actions themselves. The practical tools that we will soon give you are all taken from cognitive psychotherapy.

A new way of looking at pain
Acting in a different way than usual can be difficult

because it evokes thoughts and emotions in us that we're not used to handling. These thoughts and emotions can sometimes be so difficult, even painful, that we quickly revert to the behavior we have long been accustomed to.

In the previous chapter we speculated about what would happen if Matthew forced himself to continue seeing his potential partner even after the third date. We decided that he would feel strong unease. He experiences this unease as a form of mental pain. Matthew is accustomed to breaking off his relationships when the pain reaches a certain level.

If Matthew wants to change his situation he has to look at his pain in a new way. The pain/unease he feels consists of thoughts and emotions that arise when he gets close to another person. The pain is not, as his relationship model says, a foreboding of impending catastrophe. On the contrary, the pain is a sign that he is approaching a potential relationship. If Matthew wants to create a close, lasting relationship, he must therefore resist the impulse to combat the pain. This may be unpleasant in the short term, but it only consists of thoughts and emotions and is thus quite harmless. Matthew can therefore learn to consider this unpleasantness as a price he's willing to pay to reach the goal of getting close to another person.

Of course, this does not mean that it is constant suffering to enter into a relationship. But it is not possible to form relationships, or to live in a relationship for that matter, without sometimes experiencing troublesome emotions. If we can't handle these, it doesn't matter whether we are floating on little clouds of happiness 99% of the time. Our relationship models are still going to perceive the remaining painful 1% as a signal that danger threatens and then we will do drastic things to relieve the pain, at the price that we are again cast out into loneliness. The short-term benefit becomes minimal and the long-term loss enormous. But our control system does not take this into account.

If we manage to handle the painful elements of love in a constructive manner, we create intimacy that our inner relationship model did not believe was possible. Then the relationship model will eventually have to change. We will become more secure and have an easier time forming close relationships in the future.

The First Tool: The Do-the-Opposite Method

Now we'll introduce the first tool. It's called the do-the-opposite method and is based on the idea that in certain defined situations you actively put your relationship model aside and act contrary to what you experience as reasonable, wise and safe. The do-the-opposite method is the most important of the six tools we are going to give you. You could actually say that the remaining five tools are all there to help you use the do-the-opposite method in various ways.

When you make use of the do-the-opposite method you break loose your actions from thoughts and emotions. You decide to act in a certain way in the situation, regardless of what you think or feel in the situation itself. You consider the thoughts and feelings that arise as a price you're willing to pay so that you can experience something completely new.

The first step: Analyze a situation

Start by thinking about what you usually do when you enter the relationship staircase. In Chapter 5 we described some of the many problems that may arise on the staircase. Perhaps you recognize yourself in one or more examples, or else you have your own variation.

Then try to find a specific situation where you know that your actions cause problems for you. When you've found that kind of situation, then you can do what's called a situation analysis. You do this by filling out a form with six boxes. Below you'll see how Marcus filled in his form. Let's go through this, box by box.

Situation Analysis (Marcus)

1.	Problematic situation	Someone invites me to a party/ on a date.
2.	What do you think?	That I don't really want to go. It's going to be really boring.
3.	What do you feel?	Worry, stress.
4.	What do you do?	Decline the invitation.
5.	Short-term benefit	Become calm.
6.	Long-term consequence	Miss a chance. Remain alone. Think badly about myself.

The First Box

The problems on the relationship staircase tend to arise in a specific situation. We may of course have problems in several different types of situations, but when we use the do-the-opposite method, we break down individual situations and handle them on their own. Marcus is tired of being single but avoids situations where he might meet people he doesn't know. In the first square, Marcus defines a typical situation: He is invited to a party.

The Second Box
The problematic situation provokes thoughts. These should be described in the next box. Marcus thinks he really doesn't want to go to that party (or on that date), because he doesn't think anything fun will happen.

The Third Box
The situation also provokes emotions. Marcus writes that he feels worried and stressed.

The Fourth Box
Here Marcus describes what he does in the situation. He declines the invitation and stays home instead of going to the party/on the date.

The Fifth Box
Here Marcus fills in the short-term benefits that his actions create. Sometimes it can be tricky to discover the benefit, but there is always some type of benefit in what we do; otherwise we would have acted in a different way. Often this benefit concerns avoiding various types of troublesome emotions. Marcus' short-term benefit in staying home is that his worry goes away. He becomes calm and thinks it's nice to be by himself.

The Sixth Box
Here Marcus fills in the long-term consequences of the action. These are negative, otherwise there would have been no reason to be dissatisfied with the action. Marcus writes that the long-term consequence of staying at

home is that he remains alone, and that he feels a sense of failure because he's missed out on yet another chance to meet someone.

Now it's your turn to fill out the empty form below. If you don't want to write in the book, write on a sheet of paper or on your computer. Of course you can also keep the answers in your head if you prefer. The main thing is that you come up with at least one situation that you don't think works as well as you want. You don't need to fill in the boxes in numerical order. Sometimes it's easier to start by describing a troublesome emotion in the third box and then find a situation where this emotion usually comes up.

At the end of the book is an appendix with more empty forms if you need them.

Situation Analysis

1.	Problematic situation	
2.	What do you think?	
3.	What do you feel?	
4.	What do you do?	
5.	Short-term benefit	
6.	Long-term consequence	

The second step: Find your opposite situation
When the form is filled out and you have at least one

situation to work with, you should look at the fourth box. There your action is described. The idea of doing the opposite method is that in the future you will consciously do the exact opposite of what is in that box.

It's not the intention that you should change all your behaviors. Even if you've thought of more problematic situations, it's most effective if you decide on one situation and over time, as consistently as possible, do the opposite in that particular situation. Later you can change to a new situation to experiment with.

There are many situations where it works well to use the Do-the-Opposite method. Below are a few examples.

Old Behavior	Opposite Behavior
I often have sex the first night. Afraid that otherwise it won't be good enough; feel forced and pressured.	I decide not to have sex until after one week (or a few months), regardless of how it feels.
I talk about myself uninterruptedly.	I decide to listen and ask questions, even at the risk of creating a silence that makes me worried.
I tell too many personal things about myself, much too soon.	I decide to focus on the other person and be curious about him or her, however awkward and unusual that may feel.
I present my whole amazing CV and brag about my achievements.	I decide to talk about at least one strongly emotional memory, however unpleasant it may feel.
I get stiff and blocked, because I don't want to reveal how nervous I am.	I decide to start the date by admitting that I'm nervous, however crazy that may sound.

I have no imagination, so when I invite someone on a date it often turns out boring.	Next time I'll do something fun with my date. We'll go on an all-day outing some place we've never been, a wine-tasting, soccer match, dance class or something like that. I'll take the initiative, regardless of how exposed it may cause me to feel, and regardless of how much I worry it won't be fun.
I put such great demands on myself when I ask someone out/invite someone home that it becomes difficult and tiresome. I always have to dress perfectly and go to the best restaurant.	Next time I'll force myself to invite my date to a pizzeria and I'll go dressed in running pants and a T-shirt, however hopeless that may feel.
I'm afraid to be rejected and for that reason I don't risk talking with anyone at the bar.	I decide I have to talk with five people before I go home. The conversations can be about anything at all, and my emotions and thoughts about the project will not play a part.
I suggested an activity, but got a no. For that reason I don't suggest any more activities because it's unpleasant to be rejected.	I carefully investigate why he or she didn't want to do what I suggest. For a while, I continue making new suggestions, regardless of how rejected I feel.
I often bring a few friends along when I'm going to see someone I'm interested in. Otherwise I feel too many demands to have to be interesting.	Next time I'll invite the person home with me so that we can be completely alone, regardless of how uncertain I'm going to feel.

I often turn down invitations or say no when someone is interested in meeting, even though I regret it later.	I decide to never turn down any such invitations, whatever I think and feel about them.
I get worried when I talk with unfamiliar people.	I decide that every time I go shopping I have to say a few words to the person at the cash register, regardless of how it feels. Talking about the weather is fine.
I don't want to seem too eager and pretend not to care about what impression my date has of me. I usually prefer to dress down when I go on a date.	Next time I'll dress up like never before and start the date by clarifying how much I like the person in question.

What happens when you do the opposite?

By experimenting with the Do-the-Opposite method, you consciously go against what your relationship model says, and this is going to have consequences. The troublesome thoughts and feelings in Boxes 2 and 3 in your situation analysis are not going to disappear. Instead they will be reinforced, because your relationship model thinks that you're exposing yourself to danger and it is going to try, more and more vocally, to get you to control the situation in the old way. The more you dig in your heels and do the opposite, the more exposed you're going to feel, and your thoughts and emotions are going to become even more troublesome. The short-term benefit in Box 5 is thus not going to appear.

The point of the do-the-opposite method is to constantly focus on what you actually do. You do the opposite—regardless of what you think about it at the moment, and regardless of how it feels. You simply do not allow your thoughts and emotions to control your actions. This is probably not going to create any immediate change in your life. But when you consciously experiment with breaking old patterns, you plant a seed in your awareness, and in time that seed may create major changes. Our brains function in such a way that we can add new information, learn new ways of thinking and gather new experiences, but never consciously erase what we've added at any time. Every time you attempt to use the do-the-opposite method, you will tangibly demonstrate to your awareness that it is possible to handle habitual situations in a different way than you're accustomed to. Then one day in the future, when you're in a situation where your actions really may make a major difference, you may suddenly remember that you really are free to do something other than what your first impulse says. At that moment, the work you put into experimenting with the do-the-opposite method will pay off. The seed you planted inside yourself may then change your whole life.

All that is required for this to happen is that you train yourself in doing the opposite in those situations you've chosen, even if at the moment it doesn't seem to lead to anything at all. Be patient. That is how creating change works.

The Second Tool: The Car Ride

It may be that the Do-the-Opposite method arouses such strong emotions in you that you have to interrupt the exercise again and again and revert to your old behavior. In such a case, you can try to complement this with a tool that we call the Car Ride. It is designed to handle all the troublesome thoughts and emotions that show up.

Before you enter into a situation where you've decided to do the opposite, imagine that you're getting into a car and going out for a long drive. Imagine that the ride goes to a place you've always wanted to go and you've decided to go there regardless of how difficult the journey gets.

Now and then road signs whizz past outside the windows of the car. You can clearly see what is on the signs. Many of them inform you that for various reasons it is necessary to turn off the road or stop driving. The car ride represents your journey toward developing new experiences with the help of the do-the-opposite method. The signs represent the thoughts and the emotions that arise once you go against your old controlling behaviors. Your goal is to continue driving—that is, to complete your do-the-opposite exercise—regardless of what's on the signs. Don't avoid looking at the signs, and perhaps even read them with interest. But never do as they say.

Matthew drives the car

Let's say that it's Matthew who is sitting in the car. He's met a new partner and they've gone out three times. A week ago, they agreed to get together for the fourth time. Back then he thought it sounded like a good idea, but as the date now approaches he's starting to get hesitant. Matthew recognizes this phenomenon very well—he is starting to doubt that the partner is right once they've been together a few times. The doubt usually leads to

Matthew breaking off contact after a while. Matthew knows that the only way to get anywhere on the relationship staircase is by exposing himself to more meetings with the potential partner, even though that feels wrong. Actually it always feels wrong. For that reason he has decided to use the do-the-opposite method and see his potential partner for a fourth date, regardless of what he thinks and feels at any given moment before the meeting.

When the day of the date arrives, Matthew imagines that he is sitting in the car with a steady hold on the steering wheel. Suddenly at the side of the road a sign appears that says, "You don't belong together." Then he sees a sign with the text, "This date is going to be awkward." Going forward seems uncertain, and Matthew feels a strong need to control the situation. In normal cases he would have turned off the road by calling off the date. But now he's decided to use a different type of control. He continues forward without letting the signs influence his actions. While the car moves ahead through the night, one sign after another whizzes past outside in the darkness. Matthew reads them all, but he is careful not to allow them to affect his driving.

The longer he drives without following the signs' instructions, the more dramatic they get. Perhaps it says that the partner he's going to see is boring, that he feels suffocated by the attention, that he's not turned on sexually by her or that he doesn't really want a relationship at all. There is no limit to what Matthew's relationship model can think of to get him off the road.

But when Matthew is finally sitting face to face with his date, it's not anywhere near as terrible as he had imagined. If he is still full of thoughts about the partner's shortcomings, he goes back to the image of the car trip. He can then allow his critical thoughts to remain on the signs by the side of the road, and concentrate on making the best of the situation. There is a chance that the date will be fun and pleasant. Matthew might even fall in love.

Lena drives the car

What is on the signs depends naturally on who we are and in what situation we use the do-the-opposite method. Let's say it's Lena who's sitting in the car. Lena has met a new date a few times and in three days they'll get together again. Lena feels like she's in love and thinks a lot about the man she has met. But she also feels a strong worry that he will disappear. She often gets the impulse to contact him to check that he's not getting tired of her. However, Lena knows from before that sometimes she can scare people away by demanding too much intimacy too early. Therefore she has decided to do the opposite. She will enjoy the attraction and not make contact until the three days have passed. This is her do-the-opposite exercise.

Lena imagines that she's in the car. Suddenly Lena sees a sign with the text, "He's unreliable." The next sign reads, "Perhaps he's seeing other people." Then comes a warning sign: "Danger—Turn Off."

Lena's fear hurts so much that normally she would have done anything to be rid of the pain. For example, she might have called up her date and demanded to see him immediately. This would have soothed her fear temporarily, but it would have also meant that she had unleashed her old control mechanisms.

Instead she's holding onto the steering wheel and reading the signs. There may be some difficult, perhaps even painful days along the way. But if Lena reminds herself of where she's headed and concentrates on the task, she can leave the signs without taking action and still reach her goal.

Signs to watch out for

Regardless of what is written on these particular signs, they are going to bombard you with thoughts and emotions whose only purpose is to get you to return to your old behavior. Then it's important to hang onto the steering wheel. Definitely try not to ignore the signs, for then it will be easier for their message to ensnare you. Instead take note of what is on them. Perhaps you can even see a humorous aspect in some of the wording. When our relationship models are in revolt, they often deliver violently exaggerated descriptions of the dangers that threaten us. When your do-the-opposite exercise is over, you can think about how the thoughts and emotions that passed by are connected to your relationship model. What do they say about your view of others and your way of handling intimacy?

During the course of the journey, a number of signs are going to seem so believable that they risk getting you to automatically turn the wheel and drive off the road. Let's give you a few examples of signs that you ought to be extra cautious about.

The "this isn't working" sign

This kind of treacherous sign reads: "This is never going to work, cancel the whole exercise." This sign—or this thought, rather—insists that none of what is in this book is going to help you create a relationship and therefore it's a waste of time to try. Don't be fooled. This sign is constructed by your relationship model and it shows up because you're on the right road. Just keep driving.

The "I don't feel anything for my partner" sign

This sign maintains that you have no feelings for the person you're seeing and for that reason you ought to break off contact. This sign shows up because in your attempts to block the dangerous intimacy and thereby reduce the pain, you've managed to close off your feelings. This is not an indication that there is anything wrong with the relationship that you may be on your way into. On the contrary, the mysterious absence of feelings may indicate that deep inside you are very interested in the one you're seeing. The only way to feel anything again is by exposing yourself to intimacy. Leave the sign behind you and continue driving.

The "find the right one" sign

Another treacherous signs reads, "Sure, it's good to do the opposite. But wait until you've found someone who is right for you. The person you've met now is complete-ly wrong."

Many search for someone who is "right." Few realize that this searching is actually only one of many ways to maintain control and protect yourself against pain. The one who is "right" is an imaginary individual to whom we ascribe extremely special qualities. He or she should be able to take us all the way to the third step on the relationship staircase and at the same time free us from the pain that previously prevented us from forming relationships. The "right one" should arrive like a great parent and lift us into security.

Naturally we seldom picture the right one in just that way. It's more likely perhaps that we imagine that he or she should have a particular way of acting, should look a certain way, have a certain type of job or have specific interests. But the concept of the right one is always based on a dream of magically ending up in a wonderful place without needing to undergo the effort that in reality it is going to cost to get there. Searching for the right one prevents us from creating intimacy with people of flesh and blood who are perhaps standing right next to us. We remain passive, believing that one day these problems are going to solve themselves.

Does this mean we can create a lasting love relationship with just anyone? No, of course not. A simple question to ask yourself that can help separate the wheat from the chaff is this:

Would I want to be friends with this person? YES ⊐ NO ⊐

If the answer is yes, you've found a potential dream partner. If the answer is no, you ought to be looking for someone else. Any other objections that come up inside you should be viewed with great skepticism. It's correct that different people match up differently. But for you to be able to know whether you are a match for someone, you have to move past your inner relationship model and create intimacy with the person in question. Only then can you make a realistic assessment of how well you match up. The fact is that your control system may protest more the better you match up with the one you've met. The person you judge to be completely impossible may thus very well be your true dream partner.

As you sit in your imaginary car and see the sign saying you haven't met the right person flash past outside the window, briefly question it and then drive on.

The "break up to be kind" sign
This sign reads: "It's wrong to see someone you're not certain you want to spend the rest of your life with." This is a treacherous sign because it says that it is morally superior to pull out of the relationship. But in reality this is simply yet another way for your relationship model to get you to create distance. It's rarely wrong to try being close to another person. Fear of closeness is absolutely not a reason to refrain from initiating the relationship. If only people who were absolutely certain about the future had the right to start relationships, then no relationships would be formed whatsoever. Drive on.

The Third Tool: Willingness

When you use the Do-the-Opposite method and the Car Ride tool, you are training yourself in interpreting certain negative emotions in a completely new way. Previously you have presumably experienced sadness, worry, restlessness, melancholy and similar emotions as indications that there is something wrong in the situation you find yourself in with a potential partner. Now you are opening up to the possibility that in certain situations these emotions shouldn't be resisted at all, because they are evidence that you're in the process of creating intimacy.

Reprogramming your own way of seeing painful emotions in this way may be firmly resisted, and that's not strange. Within large segments of psychology and psychiatry, mental pain has always been viewed as something that by definition ought to be eliminated. This is a correct point of view of course where depression and other serious conditions are concerned. The problem is that we've come to consider almost all mental pain as something that ought to be avoided. Today, however, the insight is growing that a certain degree of mental pain is a necessary part of every person's life. As we make our way up the relationship staircase, it's pretty common to feel fear and other unpleasant emotions. This even applies to individuals who have secure attachment styles from childhood. The difference is that someone who has a secure attachment style is better equipped to put up with these difficult emotions. He or she may therefore pass through some of the more trying phases in a relationship without needing to use so much control that the relationship is damaged.

But in order for the rest of us to learn to do the same thing, we have to train ourselves to consider our difficult thoughts as a side effect of the fact that we are developing and creating new experiences. Tools like the do-the-opposite method and the Car Ride are there to give us that training.

However, it may prove that again and again we revert to our old behaviors because we feel much too bad when we break the old patterns. We simply can't refrain from obeying what is on the signs, because we get too nervous and worried when we try. In that situation, it's time to add another tool in order to keep the car on the road. This tool is called Willingness.

In order to explain what willingness is, we must first explain the difference between pain and suffering.

- *Pain* here refers to difficult thoughts and emotions.
- *Suffering* arises when we can't create the life we want to live, because we aren't able to endure short-term pain.

Imagine that you want to see a particularly marvelous sunrise and that this requires you to take a long hike into the wilderness. The hike is strenuous and every muscle in your body is aching. The pain in your muscles is the price you have to pay in order to see the sunrise. If you'd stayed home in bed, this pain wouldn't have occurred. But then the longing to be able to experience this sunrise would have remained a frustrated longing. The inability to fulfill the dream would have led to suffering.

Imagine now that the sunrise is instead the creation of a close, lasting relationship. The journey to such a relationship is not completely pain-free. A relationship demands intimacy and intimacy leads, as we've seen, not only to us feeling seen and loved, but also to more troublesome emotions that cause us mental pain. This pain is the price we have to pay to be able to create the relationship—in the same way that we're forced to pay with muscle aches if we want to experience a beautiful wilderness. If we choose to stay at home on our solitary sofa, we can avoid experiencing painful emotions to a certain degree. But living alone and longing for intimacy entail substantial suffering. This suffering afflicts us because we aren't capable of enduring the short-term pain that it costs to leave solitude.

The fact that so many of us have problems with creating long-term relationships is to a large extent because we are not willing to endure pain in the short term. When you experiment with the do-the-opposite method you are going to expose yourself to more pain (in the form of undesired thoughts and emotions) than you are used to. The image of this process as a car ride, where your thoughts and emotions are viewed as highway signs, is one way of putting up with the increased pain, and a method for resisting the temptation to start combating the pain. Willingness is a complementary method that you can adopt if you think the pain generated by thoughts and emotions is too severe to put up with.

The Willingness Test

Willingness is a kind of suggestion technique, and however ridiculous it may seem it has proved to work not only where putting up with worry and other troublesome emotions are concerned, but with actual physical pain as well. In order to investigate how willingness works you can do a simple test.

Find a clock with a second hand and try holding your breath as long as you can. Take your time and note how long you lasted. Continue reading when you're ready.

Ready? It's tough to hold your breath, and when the air starts to run out we focus in general only on the unpleasant feeling of not getting air. After you've rested a while you can try holding your breath again, but this time you'll focus on something besides the unpleasantness.

Imagine that you have a small meter in your pocket. It's there to show how much mental or physical pain you are experiencing at the moment. Figure 10 shows how the meter may look.

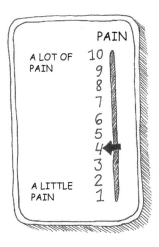

Figure 10. Imagine that in your pocket you have a meter that shows how much mental pain you're experiencing at the moment.

The stronger the pain is, the higher up the indicator moves.

When we feel bad we often put a great deal of our attention on the pain. This could be compared to keeping our eyes fixed on the pain meter. If the pain increases, we follow how the meter moves upward, millimeter by millimeter. When you held your breath and started to feel a lack of oxygen, you probably focused automatically on the discomfort you experienced. When the discomfort became too great you gave up and started breathing again.

Now imagine that you're turning over the pain meter. On the back side there is another regulator that was previously hidden. This regulator determines the degree of willingness (Figure 11).

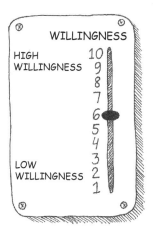

Figure 11. On the back side of the pain meter is a regulator for willingness. The higher up the regulator is pushed, the greater your readiness to put up with the pain required for you to be able to reach your long-term goal.

The degree of willingness determines what you are prepared to put up with despite the pain you are experiencing right now. The regulator can be moved up or down. By imagining that you are pushing the regulator up, you can increase your willingness. This means that you can say yes to experiencing things that are unpleasant and painful.

Now try holding your breath again, but this time maximize your degree of willingness. When you've started holding your breath, shut your eyes and imagine that you have the regulator for your willingness in front of you. Imagine that you're pushing the regulator up to the maximum, and that you are thereby saying yes to all emotions that may arise when you're not breathing. Imagine that you're looking at the regulator the whole time. Perhaps you notice that it's sliding downward little by little. Imagine that you're pushing it up again. Make sure it stays at the top position the whole time. Note how long you manage to hold your breath this time and compare with your first attempt.

Done? Most people experience that it is considerably easier to hold your breath with a high willingness setting. We can make use of this effect when we use the do-the-opposite method. Let's see how this works.

Johan uses willingness

Let's take Johan as an example. He constantly doubts whether he's together with the right partner. A few months ago he started a new relationship, and he's decided to use the do-the-opposite method this time by accepting the relationship and forcing himself to plan for a future with his girlfriend, regardless of how much his thoughts and emotions sometimes protest.

One day his girlfriend asks if he wants to take a long trip with her during the summer. This causes doubt to bubble up inside Johan. He thinks that he probably isn't really enough in love and that it feels completely wrong to decide something when he's so unsure about what he wants. Johan's inner relationship model is thus starting to revolt, and the road he's figuratively driving on is lined with signs that say that all hope is lost for the relationship.

Johan's doubt is accompanied by a worry that is so strong that it causes pain inside him. He knows that the pain is going to subside if he avoids giving his girlfriend a straight answer. Then she is going to be sad and worried, and the distance between them will increase. This is the way he usually handles his pain. Johan imagines that he's sitting in the car. He knows that he needs to remain on the road so that the relationship will have a chance to develop. He can see the signs and knows that he shouldn't follow their suggestions. But not doing so hurts too much. Perhaps he feels that he must act out his worry.

What Johan does instead is to look at the regulator that shows his degree of willingness. The regulator reveals to what extent Johan is prepared to put up with the pain he is experiencing right now. The regulator shows a very low setting. Johan is not prepared to experience any pain at all and is seriously tempted to return to his old control method.

Instead, Johan imagines that he is pushing the regulator all the way up. In this way he increases his willingness. He says yes to also experiencing what is really painful. He decides that he's willing to put up with any emotions and any thoughts whatsoever, but that he is not going to turn off the road. He is now maximally willing to pay what it costs to reach his goal. And in this state of mind he can do things that previously seemed impossible—including booking tickets for this trip.

Marcus uses willingness

Let's say that Marcus is going to use the do-the-opposite method. A woman he's met has suggested they have lunch together. Marcus gets more and more nervous the closer he gets to the scheduled day. He never has lunch with anyone other than those he knows well, and on similar occasions he has backed out at the last moment. But he's decided not to do that this time.

When the day of the lunch arrives, Marcus is very worried. This worry is in itself a worrying factor. He wants to be calm and full of self-confidence on the date. But the worry does not subside and he thinks less and less of himself. Marcus struggles to forget the worry, but only gets more and more stressed the more he tries.

Marcus imagines that he is sitting in the car en route to the goal he set up. "What's she going to think?" it says on the signs he passes. And: "You're going to make a complete fool of yourself."

Marcus does not want to appear tense and worried during lunch. He therefore tries to relax, but the worry does not go away. There is a risk that he will have to interrupt the do-the-opposite method, because soon he won't be able to stand it any longer.

What Marcus can do instead is to see his willingness regulator before him. It's set at low. Marcus wants to be rid of his worry at almost any price. But now he raises the indicator as high as it will go. This means that he increases his readiness to put up with his worry. But by no means does this mean that it goes away. The worry remains, but Marcus lets it be as it is. With a high willingness setting, Marcus manages to go to lunch even though he feels slightly out of breath and his hands are sweating. He says yes to the worry and all the symptoms the worry brings with it. The signs outside the car say that he is en route to a catastrophe. But Marcus's willingness is so high that he's willing to walk right into the catastrophe with eyes open.

By working in this way with an adjusted degree of willingness, Marcus manages to go through with a lunch that he would have felt compelled to cancel otherwise. The benefits are myriad. For one thing, he gives himself and his potential partner a chance to create a relationship together. Second, he shows himself that his way of acting does not need to be controlled by his emotions. This creates change, and makes it a little easier for him to break the control of his feelings the next time. Third, he does not obey his relationship model. By doing the opposite and going to lunch, he creates a completely new experience that in time may lead to great changes in his life.

In brief, this may be a memorable lunch.

Break the vicious circle

As soon as we start trying to combat pain, the level of our willingness decreases, and the lower our willingness is, the more we want to combat pain. We end up in a vicious circle where the struggle against pain gets more intense and our degree of willingness plummets.

When you devote yourself to trying to get rid of pain, you've locked yourself into staring at the front side of the pain meter. You concentrate on how tough it is for you and this means that the pain increases the whole time. Imagine instead that you turn the meter over and check the regulator for your willingness. Where is it set? Then push the regulator up. By doing this mental operation you change your way of viewing the pain you experience, and in turn this increase your action alternatives.

The willingness regulator has a capacity to slide downward. When you experiment with the do-the-opposite method you may need to push the regulator up many times. With a little training, however, it is going to seem natural to you to encounter difficult thoughts and emotions by pushing your willingness up. The method is not limited to relationships, but works excellently in all areas in life where a short-term struggle against troublesome thoughts and emotions (or even physical pain) risks preventing you from reaching goals that are important to you.

▶ ◀

In this chapter we've talked about actions. We have also given you three tools that have helped many people take control over their actions so they can form relationships or reach other important goals. These tools are:

- **The Do-the-Opposite Method.** Make a situation analysis with the help of the form earlier in this chapter. Experiment with changing behavior in these situations.

- **The Car Ride.** When you do the opposite, many thoughts and emotions are going to arise. See the whole thing as a car ride where the thoughts and emotions are treacherous signs that you read with interest but do not obey.

- **Willingness.** You have a meter that shows how strong your mental pain is (for example in the form of worry, dissatisfaction, restlessness, skeptical thoughts etc.). On the backside of the meter is a regulator that determines your degree of willingness. When the desire to give up becomes too great, you can raise your willingness to the maximum so that you put up with the troubling emotions. Train yourself to increase your degree of willingness in various situations and see what happens.

Chapter 7:

YOUR THOUGHTS

We have said that three systems interact and shape your life: actions, thoughts, and emotions (Figure 12). In the previous chapter we talked about actions. Now it's time to look at how your thoughts function.

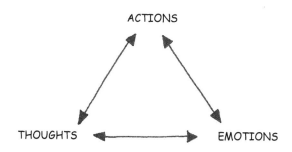

Figure 12. Everything you do and experience in life is determined by how your actions, thoughts and emotions interact.

Thinking is just carrying on an inner conversation with yourself. Thanks to this conversation, we can solve complicated problems, both the kind that exist here and now and those that may come up in the future. Thoughts are thereby an important part of the control system that helps us to ward off threats.

There are different kinds of thoughts. The type we often imagine when we hear the word are probably the reasoning, explanatory kind: "The ball is red," "The back wheel of the bicycle is rattling. Is something stuck? Best to stop and check," or perhaps even "If the Observers X and Y are at rest in relation to each other while Z moves at a high velocity in relation to X and Y, time will pass more slowly for Z as measured by X and Y."

Now however we will talk about a more specific kind of thoughts. These are called automatic thoughts and have the ability to show up instantly in our awareness before disappearing again. Characteristic of automatic thoughts is that they are sweeping and general. They assert that things are always a certain way, without nuance. This is never a matter of a longer line of reasoning, but instead refers to brief statements, key words or exclamations. Here are a few examples of what automatic thoughts may look like:

- It won't work.
- There's no point.
- I always fail.
- I can't.
- I don't have the energy.
- Boring!
- No!
- Awkward!

Automatic thoughts can also be positive:

- Exciting!
- Yes!
- Cool!

But it's usually the negative variations of automatic thoughts that create problems, so we will focus on those.

There is no way to keep from having automatic thoughts. They appear on their own and are beyond our control. Automatic thoughts are thus a part of normal life and should not be confused with having compulsory thoughts or hearing voices, which is something completely different. All people think automatic thoughts uninterruptedly, both positive and negative versions.

Often these automatic thoughts are so brief and quick that we're not even aware of them. We have heard them inside us our whole life and they have therefore become a kind of mental background noise. This does not prevent them, however, from having an enormous impact on how we interpret things that happens to us.

Automatic thoughts are not logical. Two individuals may think completely different automatic thoughts, even though they are faced with the exact same situation. Imagine for example that you are outside walking and an ambulance passes with sirens wailing. Such an event evokes automatic thoughts in most people. A few perhaps immediately think "Terrible!" and make associations with a horrendous accident. Another thinks "I'm alone!" and associates the sound with a deceased relative. A third thinks "I'm safe!" and associates the ambulance with the fact that it's nice to live in a society where we collectively see to it that everyone who needs it gets healthcare.

Thoughts create emotions

Automatic thoughts trigger emotions. Often we don't

have time to notice that we're having an automatic thought before it has gone away. But the emotion that the automatic thought released may remain longer. We then believe, incorrectly, that it is the situation we find ourselves in that creates the emotion we are experiencing. But really the emotion is the result of the automatic thoughts we've had without even noticing it.

Many automatic thoughts are useful and relevant. If you try to touch a lit candle with your finger, then probably a "No!" will flash inside you as soon as your finger approaches the flame and you feel fear. At the next moment, you've pulled your hand back before you even had time to feel the heat. The automatic thought has then filled an important function by protecting you. But negative automatic thoughts that arise in more complex contexts, such as when we're trying to find someone to fall in love with, seldom have anything to do with actual threats. That's why they create such problems.

Your inner sports commentator
In Chapter 3 we said that our relationship models contain two images:

- An image of how other people function.
- An image of how we ourselves behave in order to create intimacy.

If you chart your negative automatic thoughts in various situations, you will notice that many of them revolve around a certain theme. This theme is closely connected to the two images in the relationship model. Automatic thoughts can be described as a kind of sports commentator who lives inside us, constantly judging and commenting on all the situations we find ourselves in. The commentator uses our relationship model as a kind of rulebook that determines what the comments should sound like. The more negative images our relationship models contain, the more negative the comments become that our automatic thoughts provide us. An individual who views other people as generous and who is convinced that getting close to them will work well gets completely different comments via her automatic thoughts than someone who has learned that other people are unreliable.

Marcus has automatic thoughts

Let's look at a concrete example. Marcus's relationship model says that other people in general are not interested in him. Now he's at a party where a new acquaintance is curious and asks him to tell something about himself. At that moment the following automatic thought flashes in Marcus's mind: "Help!"

This automatic thought arises because Marcus, in his relationship model, is convinced that he is not interesting enough. This thought in turn triggers an emotion, in this case fear of failure. Marcus suddenly experiences the situation as demanding and threatening.

The automatic thought is not the result of an analysis of the actual situation. The fact that Marcus's inner commentator suddenly cries "Help!" is because his relationship model maintains that Marcus is not interesting to others. The inner commentator ignores the fact that the curious question reasonably means that someone *is* interested in him. It is Marcus's unconscious idea about how the world functions that applies, not the *actual* reality.

If a person with a completely different self-image had been asked to tell something about himself, this might have triggered an automatic thought such as "I'm interesting!" In such a case this would have led to considerably more positive emotions and the whole situation would have been experienced differently.

In Chapter 3 we described how two friends with completely different relationship models met an unknown person at the bar. Friend A became happy and open, while Friend B became cautious and more closed. The difference is due to the fact that their automatic thoughts comment on the situation based on completely different rules. Friend A has a secure attachment style and is filled by the automatic thought "Exciting!" when the new person enters the room, which in turn provokes curiosity. Friend B has an insecure attachment style and thereby has a rule system that says that new acquaintances entail onerous demands to perform. This releases the automatic thought "Hard work!" which in turn creates a feeling of worry. Both friends' automatic thoughts cause them to react differently, even though they are in the exact same situation.

Thoughts stick

If we aren't aware that there are things called automatic thoughts (which most of us who haven't been in cognitive psychotherapy are not), they can wreak havoc in our lives. We then believe that emotions that arise in difficult situations are connected to the situation itself and therefore nothing can be done about them. For example, we may dismiss a potential partner because it "doesn't feel right" when we see him or her, without understanding that the situation could have aroused completely different emotions if only our automatic thoughts looked different.

The result of this is that we need to break the control of automatic thoughts over our lives if we want to be able to take advantage of the opportunities that actually exist.

This, however, is not particularly easy. For example, it doesn't work to get rid of automatic thoughts by trying to refuse to have them. Instead, the thought gets stronger and has greater effect. You can investigate this phenomenon yourself by doing the following simple exercise.

- Think of the word "nervous."
- Try now for two minutes (watch the time) to refrain from thinking about the word "nervous." You may think about any other word, but the word "nervous" is forbidden. Imagine that you will win a hundred thousand dollars if you go two minutes without thinking of the word "nervous" a single time. Start now.

Done? You probably thought the forbidden word a number of times. For most people it's completely impossible to consciously delete a thought. When we try it only leads to us thinking it even more often.

The fact is that many people feel a little nervous when they try to refrain from thinking the word "nervous." This is due to the fact that thoughts always trigger emotions, even when it concerns thoughts that we are only thinking because a book like this encourages us to do so. So it's not strange that Marcus becomes afraid as he's sitting there with his date. At the moment he's thinking the automatic thought "Help!" he can be nothing other than afraid.

There are two ways to break the influence of automatic thoughts over your actions. The first way is to use the Car Ride tool that we described in the last chapter. Thoughts, including rapid automatic thoughts, then turn into road signs that we pass without taking action during our journey toward the goal.

It may happen, however, that certain thoughts appear so convincing that despite valiant efforts we still allow ourselves to be dragged along and convinced by them. In such cases there is yet another method to try.

The Fourth Tool: Get to Know Your Automatic Thoughts

The fourth tool is called Get to Know Your Automatic Thoughts. It is a complement to the Car Ride tool, and is there to help you place the thoughts where they belong, on the signs outside the car.

This tool is taken from cognitive therapy. There the focus for many years has been on finding ways to handle and neutralize automatic thoughts. This is of course where this whole form of therapy got its name; the word "cognitive" comes from "cognition," which means "thought."

Getting to know your automatic thoughts happens in four stages:

1. You become aware of the automatic thought.
2. You question the truth of the thought.
3. You investigate what emotion the automatic thought provokes.
4. You look for alternative thoughts that may provoke alternative emotions.

Let's see how this works in practice.

Maria has problems with the fact that she adapts herself so much to her partner that she becomes invisible. She met a new guy a few months ago and has decided to use the do-the-opposite method to train herself in talking about what she herself wants. However, this proves to be difficult. As soon as she ends up in a situation where the boyfriend suggests something that Maria isn't really excited about, she adapts even though she's decided not to.

When Maria makes a situation analysis in the way we describe earlier, the form looks like this:

Situation Analysis (Maria)

1.	Situation	He suggests a trip to Thailand.
2.	What do you think?	I don't want to, but I can't say no.
3.	What do you feel?	Feel worry, stress, sadness.
4.	What do you do?	Say yes, pretend to be enthusiastic.
5.	Short-term benefit	Become calm, because I've adapted myself to my partner.

6.	Long-term consequence	I've erased my own desire, feel bad because I go along with things I really don't want. I become invisible in the relationship.

Maria is trying to change the action in Box Four, but doesn't succeed as well as she wants. What she can do now is to look more closely at the thoughts in the second box. She thinks: "I don't want to [travel to Thailand], but I can't say no."

The next step is to *question the thought*. This happens so that she critically analyzes whether her thought "I can't say no" is truly motivated. The trick is to find as many critical questions as possible, more or less as if she were a prosecutor and the thought in the second box was the defendant. Here are a few examples of critical questions.

- *Can* I really not say no?
- Does this mean that no one is allowed to say no to others' suggestions, or does the rule only apply to me?
- In that case, why?
- If my friend had told me that she doesn't think she has the right to say no to suggestions from her boyfriend, what would I have said to her?
- What is the worst thing that can happen if I expressed a different desire?
- What benefits would that entail?
- What do I think personally about people who express what they think? Do I want to push them away from me or do I appreciate associating with them?

When Maria has critically analyzed her thoughts it's time to create so-called *alternative thoughts*. The way this works is that she asks herself what she most would have wanted to think in that situation.

Maria decides that her alternative thought reads: "Of course I have the right to express my opinion." She notes this to the right of the second box in the form (Table 2).

Then Maria thinks about what alternative emotion her alternative thought might create. She decides that she would feel strong.

Finally she thinks about what her alternative thought and emotion might lead to as an alternative behavior. In this particular situation she would say that she would prefer to travel to Greece. So this is how the form looks when she is finished:

1.	Situation	He suggests a trip to Thailand.	
2.	What do you think?	I don't want to, but I can't say no.	I have the right to say what I really think.
3.	What do you feel?	Feel worry, stress, sadness.	Feeling of strength.
4	What do you do?	Say yes, pretend to be enthusiastic.	Say that I would rather go to Greece.

5.	Short-term benefit	Become calm, because I've adapted myself	Stress.
6.	Long-term consequence	I've erased my own desire, feel bad because I go along with things that I don't really want. I become invisible in the relationship.	Get a higher value because I say what I want. I become visible in the relationship.

Table 2. Situation analysis. Maria notes her alternative thoughts, emotions and actions to the right of Boxes Two, Three and Four.

At the end of this book there is a blank form for you to use. By doing this exercise you will become more aware of the role your automatic thoughts play. This will make it possible for you to discover them and handle them with a certain degree of distance. The next time you find yourself in a tricky situation, you're going to be prepared in a different way than before and the risk will therefore be less that you will simply do as you usually do out of inertia. When you nonetheless *do* fall back into old behaviors, which is naturally going to happen, you can fill out the form again and analyze exactly what happened. This will increase your preparedness next time. This is how long-term change is created.

Chapter 8:

YOUR EMOTIONS

We have now talked about your actions and your thoughts, so only one system remains to be discussed in the triangle of systems that guides your life (Figure 13). This is the system of your emotions, and it is at least as important a system as the other two.

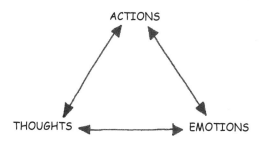

Figure 13. The three systems—actions, thoughts and emotions—interact in everything you do and everything you are part of.

Emotions are the most fundamental of the three systems. We cannot use our thoughts until the left half of the brain has grown and we have developed a language. But emotions we have with us right from birth. Despite this, most of us are not particularly good at under-standing and handling our emotions. For that reason, let's have a basic refresher of what emotions are.

For a long time it was believed that emotions were insignificant compared with thoughts, but modern brain research has shown that this is completely wrong. Emotions are actually the prerequisite for us being able to experience that we are alive. A life without emotions would thus not be experienced as a life whatsoever.

There are nine so-called basic emotions. Throughout the development of the human race, these nine emo-tions have informed us of how our bodies are doing, warned of threats and triggered various types of behav-iors that increased our chances of surviving. Below is a list of these nine basic emotions. In the columns to the right you see which behaviors the various emotions trigger, and what function the emotion serves in our lives.

Emotion	Example of How the Emo-tion Causes You to Act	Why Does the Emotion Exist?
Interest (includes curiosity, attraction, etc.)	You want to get close to something or someone; try out and investigate.	The emotion of inter-est makes you want to get closer to what may be beneficial for you.
Happiness (also pride, love, ecsta-sy, etc.)	You remain in the situa-tion and continue what you're doing.	Happiness makes you want to stay in situ-ations that are good for you.
Surprise	You stop and reflect.	Surprise makes you stop and reconsider your way of looking at life so that you can take in new information.
Fear, worry	You flee, seek shelter, seek help or remain passive.	Fear makes you avoid dangers.

Sorrow, low spirits	You withdraw, become passive, cry, brood.	Sorrow makes you take time for necessary reflection. It also makes you want to hold on to things that are valuable to you when you risk losing them.
Shame	You abruptly stop being happy and/or interested and instead want to hide or simply vanish into a hole in the ground. You may want to criticize yourself too harshly, or even attack your surroundings.	Shame keeps you from being so intoxicated by happiness and curiosity that you violate social rules or cross others' boundaries.
Anger, irritation	You attack your surroundings physically or verbally.	Anger protects you by motivating you to protect yourself against threats.
Aversion	You increase distance or try to get rid of what you feel averse to. Arises when you smell rotten, inedible food.	Aversion protects you from eating bad food.
Disgust	You spit and grimace. Arises when you eat something you thought would taste good but that tastes bad.	Disgust protects you from consuming things that are harmful to eat or drink.

Table 3. The nine basic emotions. The compilation is partly from the book KBT i utveckling (Cognitive Behavior Therapy in Development) by Anna Kåver (Stockholm, Natur & Kultur, 2006).

These nine emotions already exist within us when we are infants and we need them to be able to develop. For example, when an infant looks at a piece of rustling newsprint, the emotion of *curiosity* arises and therefore the child will want to investigate the paper. Curiosity is an emotion that is necessary for the child to want to investigate the world around her, which is a prerequisite for her development. In the same way the emotion of *surprise* contributes to making the child open to new information, while *happiness* causes the child to want to continue doing the kinds of things that cause it to feel good. When a nine-month-old baby has crawled too far away from her parents, the child feels fear. This fear is a warning signal that causes the child to want to make her way back to her parents. In the same way, the emotions of *aversion* and *disgust* keep the child from eating things that may be poisonous. All the basic emotions have important functions early in our lives.

When you were a newborn your life consisted almost entirely of emotions. By turns you were furious, sad, happy and so on, depending on what you were involved in. You personally experienced that emotions were something that struck you like lightning from a clear blue sky, completely outside your control. In order to become a functioning person you needed to learn to weave emotions together with thoughts. Here your parents (or other adults who took care of you) were your teachers. When you were sad they might say, "You're sad because you're tired. We'll take a walk with the stroller so you can sleep a little." When you laughed out loud on the roller coaster they might have said "Look how much you like riding the roller coaster!" What your parents were doing then, whether they realized it or not, was to instinctively help you weave together emotional experiences with appropriate thoughts. By constantly interpreting emotions with words, they demonstrated to you that every emotion has a name and that by means of thoughts you can both explain what is causing the emotion and decide what action you should adopt to change the emotion.

In time you started to construct thoughts yourself and used them to handle emotions the way your parents taught you. When you felt sad, instead of simply crying you could think that the unpleasant emotion was perhaps due to the fact that you hadn't eaten for a long time, and then signal to your parents that you needed food. The older you became, the more training you got in connecting specific emotions with right thoughts and thereby also with suitable actions, which meant that you could handle increasingly complex contexts on your own.

As adults we all have a unique way of weaving together actions, thoughts and emotions. You might say that our personalities are determined by how this interaction functions. How good we got at getting our weaving to function depends on how capable our teachers were. If our parents could take their own emotions seriously and were skilled at weaving them together with constructive thoughts and actions, then we too likely became good at that. Many of us, however, grew up with parents who did not handle emotions in a particularly successful way. Perhaps they couldn't stand it when we were sad or angry, and taught us to avoid such emotions.

This has led to it being difficult for many of us to name the emotions we have inside us and connect them with constructive thoughts. If we talk about emotions at all, we often use a throng of concepts that do not always correctly describe what we're actually feeling.

Below you will see a number of examples of such

expressions. At the top of each column you will see the basic emotion that the concepts originally stood for (Table 4).

As you see, a number of concepts conceal the underlying emotion rather than bring it into the light. Sometimes this may be the purpose. It is more socially acceptable to say that a heavy work load makes you "worried" or perhaps even "stressed" than to explain that you're simply *afraid*, in this case of not managing the assignment. In the same way it may be easier to say that you're disappointed in someone than to describe the emotion of sorrow that is behind all disappointments. But by avoiding calling our emotions by their right names, we make it more difficult for us to weave them together with thoughts and actions that can help us to feel better.

Afraid	Angry	Sad	Happy	Ashamed
Tense	Irritated	Down	Satisfied	Embar-rassed
Anxious	Bored	Tired	Content	Afraid
Worried	"Crazy"	Unhappy	Good mood	Shy
Nervous	Bitter	De-pressed	Cheerful	Awkward
"Stressed"	Upset	Joyless	Elated	Regretful
Worried	Hateful	Aban-doned	Enthusi-astic	
Uncertain	Hostile	Disap-pointed	Delighted	Dumb
Terrified	Destruc-tive	Gloomy	Eager	"I feel like an idiot"

Frightened		Miserable	Ecstatic	
"That's gross"			Proud	

Table 4. Examples of words that we use when we are actually talking about basic emotions. (Source: Giacomo d'Elia, Det kognitiva samtalet i vården [The Cognitive Dialogue in Healthcare], Natur & Kultur, 2004.)

A common way of concealing emotions from yourself is to mix them together with thoughts. We may say, for example, "I feel like I'm not keeping up." But then we're actually expressing not an emotion but a *thought* that says, "I'm not keeping up." The emotion that is *connected* to the thought is fear. The formulation "I feel like I'm not keeping up" may thus be a way to avoid becoming aware of a fear that we perhaps have a hard time handling. In the same way, the sentence "I feel like he doesn't like me" is a mixture of thoughts and emotions. "She doesn't like me" is a *thought.* Here too the emotion that is connected with the thought is fear: the fear of not being good enough, the fear of not being worthy of being loved. But the emotion becomes invisible, as long as we believe that it is a thought.

Avoiding negative emotions

Many of the problems we are faced with in our lives are connected to our attempts to avoid experiencing any negative emotions whatsoever. We already learned this as small children from our parents, who once upon a time learned the same thing from their parents. And so we try to adapt our way of living so that negative emotions won't be released.

Take Maria, for example, the woman who always adapts herself to her partner. When she was little, Maria learned that her parents couldn't stand it when she was sad. This led to her weaving together the emotion of sadness with the thought "I'm worthless," which in turn released the emotions of shame, fear and even more sadness. If Maria's parents had been better at handling emotions, perhaps they would have been able to teach their daughter instead to weave together sadness with the thought "I'm sad, why is that?" Sadness would then have become a valuable signal of Maria's inner state and would have made it possible for her to change the circumstance that was making her sad.

But instead Maria learned to conceal the sadness, both from herself and from people around her. After having trained herself in this during her entire upbringing, as an adult she can hardly identify any emotions other than happiness and curiosity. But all of the troublesome emotions are of course still there inside her, and her relationships are damaged by the fact that she is not able to show them.

If you've learned to avoid negative emotions, you often automatically assume that there is something wrong with the situations where negative emotions arise. If for example we feel worry—a milder form of fear—when we meet a potential partner, then perhaps we say afterwards to a friend that it "didn't feel right." The only emotions that we might approve during a date are then happiness and curiosity. The problem is that close relationships almost always create both positive and negative emotions. This is the basic premise of love:

It gives us the greatest enjoyment and happiness, but also a good deal of pain—and we can't have one without the other. The only way to completely avoid difficult emotions is to avoid lasting relationships completely—and that is what many people do in practice when they devote years to looking for a pain-free relationship.

Another way of avoiding negative emotions is to turn to various types of addiction. Alcohol or drug abuse, being a workaholic, exercise addiction, sex addiction and various forms of eating disorders are all effective methods of eliminating undesired emotions in the short term. But in the longer perspective of course, many new and greater problems are created.

Learn to identify emotions

Emotions are an important signaling system that let us know how we're doing and trigger thoughts and actions with which we can change and develop our lives and ourselves. But in order for this interaction to be able to function in a good way, we must be able to identify our emotions. If we didn't get good enough at this as children, we can work on this capacity as adults.

If you want you can now do a simple test where you investigate the emotions that are inside you right now. You've now read to this point in the book, and it may therefore be interesting to know what emotions this reading evokes in you.

Do the following: When you've finished reading the instructions below, set aside the book, close your eyes and focus on what you're feeling right now. Also investigate the emotions that are felt in various places in your body. You see, an emotion always leads to a physical reaction. Whether we're happy, curious, scared, angry or filled with some other emotion, it affects our way of breathing, our posture, our way of speaking and even how we smell—and some emotions even cause us to secrete chemical substances through our skin.

So check to see whether you are tense or relaxed. How does your back feel? Your shoulders? Your jaws? How does it feel in your stomach? How about breathing? Do your breaths go deep down into your belly or do they remain high up in the chest? Ask yourself what emotion the physical sensations you discover might belong to.

Also investigate your thoughts. In the last chapter we said that all thoughts trigger emotions. But it is also the case that all emotions trigger new thoughts (which in turn trigger even more emotions, which lead to even more thoughts, and so on—the systems constantly cross-pollinate each other). Ask yourself whether any of the thoughts you're having right now may originate from an emotion, and in that case what the emotion is. Also consider whether by thinking a certain thought you are *avoiding* any particular undesired emotion.

When you've found an emotion, then you can continue the exercise by judging the intensity of the emotion. Let's say that you're feeling worried, which is a form of fear. Think about how strong the worry is. How would it feel if you were even a little more worried? How worried are you in relation to the terror you would have felt at the news of a possible fatal cancer you'd been tested for?

Before you start the exercise, perhaps you want to look through the list of emotions earlier in this chapter (Table 3). It may make it easier for you to put names on the emotions you discover. Then it's just a matter of doing the exercise.

The difference between emotions and actions

If you did the exercise, perhaps you thought it felt unusual to focus on your emotions in this way. Many of us devote considerable energy to avoiding experiencing emotions. One reason for this may be that we think that emotions will trigger behaviors that we have learned are unacceptable. Perhaps we imagine that the emotion *sorrow* is connected with the phenomenon "crying all night long and not being able to stop." Perhaps we associate wrath with violence, or with breaking off connections with people around us. These associations between emotions and actions are an unfortunate result of our upbringing. Perhaps our parents reacted equally judgmentally when we expressed fury as if we had physically attacked them. In reality it is one thing to experience emotions and a completely different thing to act. It may therefore be interesting to think about how great a difference there is between *feeling* and *acting*. When in the future you feel sad, you can investigate how the sadness feels in the muscles of your body, in your stomach and in your way of breathing. Imagine the behavior that you associate with the emotion and note that it's not at all necessary to act in that way simply because you've allowed yourself to *feel* the emotion.

Training yourself to handle emotions in this way is not difficult and doesn't take much time. All that is required is that now and then you give your emotions a certain degree of attention. The reward is that you will more easily be able to experiment with the Do-the-Opposite method and the Car Ride tool that we talked about in Chapter 6. When you break old behaviors, your proficiency in handling emotions is going to make it easier for you to see what emotions are zooming past.

It will also be easier for you to resist the impulse to let your emotions govern you in the way you're used to.

The necessity of communicating emotions

For us to be able to handle emotions in a constructive manner, it's not enough that we can experience and name them ourselves. We also need to be able to explain to others what we're feeling. When you've come a little farther up on the relationship staircase, this is a completely necessary proficiency. A relationship where the parties can't express their emotions cannot be deepened, and instead stagnates in its initial stage where the intimacy has a difficult time developing.

But many of us have a hard time expressing even positive emotions that we have for other people. Perhaps we've learned not to be too eager and we therefore try to act disinterested, even if we've met someone who arouses strong interest in us.

If you know that you are usually stingy with appreciation, then simply try to express what you feel for someone that you like and do it even if it goes against your code of behavior. Tell the other person that it felt good to see him or her the last time you met. Say that you are eager to get together again. Investigate what happens inside you when you reveal your positive emotions. Perhaps it doesn't feel quite as strange as you thought it would.

The next step is to train yourself in expressing negative emotions. However much it goes against the grain, say it like this: "I got really nervous when you called and wanted to get together again"; "I got worried when you couldn't see me last Thursday"; "I've been looking forward to seeing you again, but at the same time I feel a little scared." Investigate what happens between you when you express these emotions. How is your (potential) partner's behavior affected? How do you feel personally when you open up a little?

The Fifth Tool: Little Person and Big Person

Being able to understand and name your emotions is of great help when you have to make choices, not least where relationships are concerned. It's through our emotions that we can find out what we want deep inside. Sometimes however it may be difficult to know what our emotions are saying. Perhaps our emotions provoke so many thoughts that in the end we don't know where the emotions stop and the thoughts begin. In such situations you can use a tool called Little Person and Big Person. Its purpose is to separate emotions from thoughts.

Imagine that you have two versions of yourself inside you: The big person takes care of your thoughts and the kinds of needs you can think your way to, while the Little Person takes care of your emotional needs. In order for you to be able to function well, these two persons have to cooperate (Figure 14).

Figure 14. Imagine that you have one version of yourself inside you that is big and one that is little. The big person takes care of your thoughts. The little person takes care of your emotions.

When one of the persons takes control

The big person and the little person have varying degrees of influence over our lives, depending on how our life situation appears at the moment. A typical situation where the little person can almost entirely take control, is when we are deeply in love. Then we allow ourselves to be filled by emotions and life has an easiness that perhaps we've hardly experienced since we were children. At this point, love is seen as a fun game, and many of us experience the best moments in our lives when we find ourselves in this state.

In other situations in life the big person inside us tends to take over. This may happen, for example, when a relationship is already well established and career plans, finances and strategies for the future take more and more attention. The big person manages that sort of thing and these are of course important matters. But if we let the big person dominate our life too much, we risk not having much joy, curiosity or love left.

Ideally, the little person and the big person cooperate and are alternately allowed to dominate in situations where they are best suited. In such a way we can keep a career and take care of the practical aspects of life without losing the emotions in our relationships. But for someone who has an insecure attachment style from childhood, there may be added difficulty to get the little person and the big person to cooperate on equal terms.

In individuals with an insecure-avoidant attachment style the big person dominates, because they've learned not to listen to what the little person has to say. In individuals with *insecure-ambivalent* attachment styles it's the opposite. Here the little person dominates, while the big person has learned to be silent.

The purpose of the Little Person and Big Person tool is to get the one of the two characters who is usually silent to speak. Let's see how this might happen in practice.

Beatrice uses "Little Person and Big Person"

Beatrice is the woman who only initiates relationships as a mistress with married men and who gets bored with anyone who is more available.

Beatrice thinks it's tricky to figure out what she's feeling. When she's with her lover she feels relatively calm, but at the same time she is dissatisfied with being a mistress. On those occasions when she's tried to date an available man, she has felt both stressed and bored at the same time. It has always seemed impossible to go further with the relationship.

When Beatrice uses the Little Person and Big Person tool, she starts by imagining that the little and big Beatrices are sitting in front of her. Then she turns to the little Beatrice and asks a direct question.

What do you think about being with a married man?

After a moment of thinking Beatrice knows that the little person inside her is sad. She wants to have a partner who does not go away, and who doesn't drop her for someone else.

Now Beatrice turns to the big person.

What do you think about being with a married man?

The answer is that the big person thinks there is less risk of unpleasant surprises as long as Beatrice is with an occupied man.

The next time Beatrice meets a man who's available and who at least seems somewhat interesting, she can repeat the exercise. The first question is *What does Little Beatrice think about being with him?* The answer may very well be that the little person is eager and excited. She longs to be with someone who only loves Beatrice.

And then Beatrice turns to the big person.

What does Big Beatrice think about being with him?

The answer is that the situation is far too uncertain. It's not possible to play and have fun with an available man, because the whole time she is threatened by a painful disappointment. Big Beatrice therefore rules out the man as boring and hopeless.

Thus the big and little Beatrices find themselves in conflict with one another. Until now the big Beatrice has been allowed to make all the decisions, and the needs the little Beatrice stands for have been ignored. By actively asking herself what these two versions of her want, Beatrice can become more aware of her complete emotional needs. The exercise means that it will be harder in the future for her to set aside her need for genuine intimacy, and in time this will affect her actions. The next time she rules out an available man as worthless she is going to have a slightly easier time viewing her critical thoughts with distance. Perhaps for a moment she may hear little Beatrice's desire inside her. This may be enough for her to at least give her date one more chance before she gives up. In this manner, Beatrice will start a process that may lead to major changes.

Gustav uses "Little Person and Big Person"

Gustav is the man who has many temporary relationships, but who has a hard time sticking around. When Gustav tries to use the Do-the-Opposite method (Chapter 6), for example, by seeing a partner a few weeks without having sex, he feels strong resistance. He has a hard time figuring out what is causing the resistance and therefore he may benefit from the Little Person and Big Person tool.

After Gustav has met his date he thinks through what happened and then asks a question directly to Big Gustav.

What do you think about just socializing without having sex?

The big Gustav inside him replies that the new partner is probably fun to have sex with, but that a relationship would never work. This is exactly what Gustav is used to thinking about the ones he sees.

Gustav now turns to the little person.

What do you think about just socializing without having sex?

It may be difficult for Gustav to hear an answer. The little Gustav has led a languishing life for so many years that he's almost become mute. But Gustav persists in trying to make contact with the little person and at last he hears a faint voice that says, "I don't want to be alone, I want to be close."

Gustav needs to carefully think about how the little person inside himself is doing. In that version of himself is gathered all of his innate longing for intimacy. If he can imagine that he needs to change his way of acting because he wants to help Little Gustav to feel better, this may help him to become more decisive. This type of mental exercise may mean that he more clearly experiences his emotional needs, which is going to make it more difficult for him to allow his thoughts to take control in the way that has happened up until now. It is simply not as easy to overlook what the little person desires when the little person has finally been able to express himself freely.

Lena uses "Little Person and Big Person"

Lena is the woman who wants guarantees early on that the relationship she is initiating will be long-term and that the partner wants to have children. She can sometimes become so suspicious and clingy that she scares away the ones she's attracted to. Lena has an insecure-ambivalent attachment style. She is governed by emotions, which means that it is often the little person who controls her.

A few weeks ago Lena met a new man. She is in love and he seems to be too. They see each other often and if they don't on a particular day they always call each other when they've gone to bed. One day Lena has a lot to do and hasn't contacted her partner the whole day. When she comes home at about nine o'clock she calls him, but it appears that his cell phone is turned off. This has never happened before during their brief acquaintance. Until now Lena has been convinced that the man is in love with her. But when she can't get in touch with him, her inner relationship model awakens and says that she's in the process of being forgotten and abandoned again.

Lena calls once every ten minutes for two hours and her worry starts to turn into panic.

In this situation Lena can benefit from the Little Person and Big Person tool. She starts by turning to the little Lena that exists inside her and asking this question:

Why hasn't he tried to reach me?

Little Lena replies that a catastrophe has occurred. Either the guy has decided he's not interested in her at all and is now letting her know that by making himself unavailable, or else he's had a fatal accident. In any event they'll never see each other again. This man is just as unreliable as all the others, and even if he were to show up again it's not certain that Lena would have anything to do with him, not the way he's hurt her.

These are exactly the type of thoughts that have been rushing through Lena's head during the last few hours. Lena now turns to the big person inside her and asks the same question.

Why hasn't he tried to reach me?

The big Lena is considerably calmer than the little one. She replies that there may be less dramatic explanations for the silence. Perhaps his cell phone isn't charged, or maybe he has too much to do at work to be able to listen to voicemail. It is much too soon to draw any conclusions and therefore she ought to wait until tomorrow before she does anything.

By dividing herself into two parts in this way Lena can break the hold of her emotions for a while and instead make contact with her thoughts. This means that she has an easier time consoling herself.

After the conversation with the big, wise person inside her, Lena goes to sleep at last. She doesn't fall asleep calmly, but she isn't feeling panic either.

The following morning her partner calls. He had worked from seven in the morning until ten at night and fell asleep like a log at home on the couch before he managed to call Lena. Now he is eager to see her and wonders if they mightn't meet for lunch.

Chapter 9:

MINDFULNESS

What the tools we've presented so far have in common is that they help you observe your thoughts and emotions. In that way you don't allow them to automatically control your life.

Before we end we're going to offer one last tool. It's called *Mindfulness* and is very powerful where breaking the control of thoughts and emotions is concerned. There are those who might say that mindfulness is in the process of creating a revolution within psychotherapy right now. This is paradoxical, because it's a technique that's been used for thousands of years.

The Sixth Tool: Mindfulness

The idea of mindfulness is to train the brain, by means of various types of meditation, so that it learns to let one's awareness stay in the present, rather than be carried off by various thoughts and emotions. There is no exercise more effective where creating distance between thoughts and emotions is concerned.

The Car Ride tool (Chapter 6) is a kind of "light" version of mindfulness. The image of a car ride helps you place your thoughts and emotions on road signs outside the car as you experiment with breaking up old patterns. Mindfulness involves the same thing, but now the car's journey is your entire life.

Practicing mindfulness is not difficult. What's required is simply a bit of stubbornness. But if you're willing to invest some time we can promise you an interesting experience. In purely practical terms, the way it works is that every day you train yourself to consciously observe the emotions and thoughts that are constantly streaming through your awareness. This may sound fuzzy, but it has been shown that if you practice a while every day for a few months, this produces demonstrable changes in the brain's way of working. The training creates a different sense of reality, greater tolerance for stress, less risk of becoming depressed and a strongly increased ability to resist the old habit of being carried away by thoughts and emotions. The more you stay with it, the greater the change is going to be. Even small efforts create change, so don't let a lack of time keep you from trying.

We will give you three mindfulness exercises. The first two are intended as an introduction, while the third will create substantial changes.

Mindfulness exercise 1: Drink juice consciously

The purpose of this exercise is to give you a sense of what mindfulness is. It's done during breakfast, and it's good to try it a few mornings in a row.

The background to the exercise is that many of us are so occupied by our thoughts and/or emotions that we seldom really experience the moment in which we actually find ourselves. Our thoughts and emotions are either planning the future or going over things that happened in the past. Perhaps you take a shower in the morning and think that a cup of coffee would be nice after that. But as you're drinking your coffee, your thoughts are already at work, and when the cup is empty you're surprised that it's gone. In this way we miss out on our lives moment by moment, and in the end we may be forced to admit that we missed almost all of it.

The idea of the exercise is to drink juice (or, if you prefer, tea or coffee) with total awareness. The purpose is to demonstrate to yourself how different it feels to be present in the now. If during the exercise you think what you're doing is ridiculous, continue anyway. That idea is simply an attempt to escape being present, because sometimes this can evoke emotions we're not used to.

Do this: Imagine that you are from another planet and have never seen a glass of juice before. Your task is to experience every aspect of drinking juice with absolute presence at every moment. Start by looking at the glass. Investigate the surface of the juice at close range. If there are particles of fruit pulp on the surface, survey the pattern they create as if it were the surface of a planet. Study light reflections and other phenomena. Then sniff the juice. How does the aroma affect you?

Take plenty of time before you finally taste the juice. Note how your mouth and tongue behave in order to receive the first drops. Let a drop settle on your tongue. Note how your taste buds react. Let the first drop spread in your mouth. How does the taste change?

Next time you drink juice, perhaps out of old habit you will take several gulps of juice without even noticing that you're doing so. Perhaps you're occupied by reading the newspaper, or else your thoughts and emotions are somewhere else. When you discover what has happened, stop. Think about the difference between the experience of drinking juice during the mindfulness exercise and drinking juice in your usual way.

Mindfulness exercise 2: Open doors consciously

This is also an exercise that introduces mindfulness. The idea is that during any given day you will become completely aware of what you do as you open doors. Opening a door is one of many actions we do every day over and over again without even noticing that we're doing it. As we approach a closed door we are already on the other side of it in our minds. Afterwards we often don't even remember that we went through the door.

The way this exercise works is that you decide to be consciously present in the moment every time you open a door, during an entire day. Every time you open and close a door, you will thus do it with the exact same awareness and openness to the experience as when you drank juice. How does the handle feel against your palm and fingers? How do your arm muscles work to turn the handle? How does the air feel against your skin as the door opens? How does your body feel as it shifts balance from one leg to another in order to pass through it? How do your feet feel as you walk? Your legs? How do the various parts of your body feel as you close the door behind you?

This is harder than you may think. Again and again you are going to forget and go through a door without conscious presence. But the idea of the exercise is to keep trying.

Mindfulness exercise 3: Meditation

Most of us have so many ideas about what meditation

is that the phenomenon has acquired an air of mystery. Perhaps we associate it with bearded men sitting on mountaintops or orange-clad disciples in the lotus position around an enlightened master. Or we just think that meditation requires extensive life changes in order for us to get started.

None of this is correct. Meditation is basically a simple exercise in conscious presence that neither requires any particular circumstances nor needs to take much time. The fact is that the only way to fail with meditation is to avoid meditating. Everything that happens during meditation, including all the inner resistance that necessarily arises, is a part of the meditation process.

In order to meditate you need to find a place where you can be by yourself. Decide for how long you want to meditate. One suggestion is that you start with five to ten minutes per day and then increase the time when you think it feels right to do so. If you want, you can use a timer that signals when the meditation is over.

You can sit on a chair, on a pillow or on the floor. If you sit on a chair, you should sit a little forward on the seat so that your back does not have contact with the chair.

Then do this:

1. Sit with back straight, but not so straight that it feels stiff and uncomfortable. Try until you find a way of sitting that is both comfortable and gives you a feeling of dignity. Imagine that you are a mountain in repose.
2. Close your eyes and let your shoulders down. You can have your hands in your lap or some

other place that feels comfortable to you. If you hear sounds, then spend some time experiencing these sounds, including sounds from your own body. Then transfer your focus to how your body feels. Sense how your feet feel, how your legs/thighs press against the foundation, feel the sensations in your hands, arms, back, neck and face.

3. Then transfer your attention to your breathing. Note how it feels to exhale the breath itself. Focus on how the air feels against your nostrils as you breathe in, how it feels as the air passes the throat, how the breathing motion continues down toward the stomach. Follow the air to the navel and then the same way back out again. Breathe as normal. The trick is not to change what's happening, but to consciously observe everything that is happening. You may imagine that your breaths are like waves that strike a shore again and again and are then drawn out to sea. No wave is like another. Observe each breath with just as much concentration as if it were your very first. Do this over and over again through the entire meditation.

4. When you focus on breathing your thoughts are going to start insisting on attention. Meditation is not based, as many believe, on stopping your thoughts, which is completely impossible. The fact that thoughts steal our attention over and over again is, on the other hand, a central feature of meditation. Thoughts are handled like this:

- Suddenly you become aware that you are no longer focusing on breathing but instead on a thought or perhaps an emotion that has stolen your attention.
- Note calmly what thought or emotion it is that has taken away your attention.
- Then calmly return to full awareness of your breathing.

During the course of meditation, your thoughts are going to wander off again. That's the idea. The training is in repeatedly going through the three steps above: discovering that your thoughts have wandered, noting what thoughts/emotions they concern, and then calmly moving your focus back to the next inhalation or exhalation.

If you meditate for five minutes you may have to move your focus back once every five seconds. This means that you are going to notice a hundred times that your thoughts have drawn your attention away, and a hundred times you will have trained yourself to return focus on your breathing in the meantime. See this as if you had done one hundred repetitions on an exercise machine. The more repetitions you do, the stronger your capacity for exercising your conscious presence will become.

Among the thoughts that come up as you're meditating will be ones like "This isn't working," "What am I doing?" "I'm worthless at this," and so on. There isn't a person in the whole world who began meditating without having such thoughts over and over again. Treat these thoughts exactly like all the other thoughts: Note that they arose and calmly move your focus back to your breathing.

If you start with five minutes of meditation you can extend the time at a pace that suits you. If you get up to fifteen minutes per day, you've come a long way. If you continue to train regularly for a few months, the like-lihood is great that you are going to experience reality a little differently than you were used to. That it takes several weeks has to do with the fact that meditation changes how your brain functions and that change always requires some time.

A Relationship as an Exercise in Mindfulness

Breathing is something we do in all situations in life. If you meditate regularly for a few weeks you are going to discover that in various situations you will spontaneously notice that your thoughts and emotions have taken you away. Then you can focus on your breathing and in that way again become consciously present in the moment. This is a good thing to know in many situations, not least in connection with a date.

When you meet someone you're interested in, the pressure you may feel can cause your thoughts and emotions to end up far, far away from the encounter itself. This applies regardless of whether the relationship has recently started or if it's gone on for a while. Perhaps you're wondering whether you're going to be married in two years, if the other person is going to want to have children, if you're sufficiently interesting or if the other person is sufficiently good-looking/smart/fun and so on. Many of these thoughts evoke difficult emotions because they create a demand for performance. The result can be fear, sadness or anger. If you are carried away by these emotions, the result will be that intimacy turns into distance.

If you exercise your mindfulness with the help of the techniques above, it will be easier for you to remain in the moment. One possibility is that you make the encounter or date with your (potential) partner into a mindfulness exercise in itself. Direct all of your attention to what is happening between you. How does it feel to sit there? Experience the moment. Note how the food smells if you're eating; how the air feels if you're outside walking. If you have thoughts that have nothing to do with the context you're in, note this, but then let your thoughts be. Return your concentration to the two of you who are together right now. Let yourself be filled by what is happening between you, right now. In that way, you create the possibility of a stronger intimacy.

Chapter 10:

HOW DID THINGS WORK OUT FOR MATTHEW, MARIA AND THE OTHERS?

We will conclude by telling how things went for Matthew, Maria, Lena, Johan, Gustav, Beatrice and Marcus. When the real individuals behind these made-up names sought help with Egil, he gave them the opportunity to experiment with the tools you yourself have now been exposed to in this book:

- The Do-the-Opposite method
- The Car Ride tool
- The Willingness tool
- The Get to Know Your Automatic Thoughts tool
- The Little Person and Big Person tool
- The Mindfulness tool

All of our seven case individuals used the Do-the-Opposite method. Beyond that they selected whichever tools proved to suit them best. Let's see how it went.

Matthew

Matthew has an insecure-avoidant attachment style. He is controlled by thoughts and his problem is that by the third date he starts doubting that the person he's met is right for him. He then distances himself emotionally and physically, which means that his relationships are often damaged before they've even managed to start in earnest.

Matthew needed to train himself in staying put. He used only a single tool, and that was the Do-the-Opposite method. The exercise was that he would see his next date at least five times before he gave up.

At first it didn't feel good at all. When Matthew went on the fourth and fifth date, it felt as if he were doing violence to himself. He really had no desire for his partner. But when he tried the same thing with another person, he was forced to admit to himself that the experiment had brought something new, and in an unexpected way. By virtue of the fact that Matthew saw his date five times, his normal dating situation started to change. Previously he'd always been content with a few visits to a restaurant, but to see someone five times requires variation. Matthew invited his date on a picnic, and on one occasion he cooked food at home. This led to him being able to show more sides of himself, which meant that the whole contact felt different. He became more open and more curious than before.

Today Matthew can go on several dates without major difficulties and without his old system for avoiding intimacy starting up. For the past few months he's had a proper girlfriend. He's not sure whether it's going to last, but they socialize and enjoy each other's company regularly.

Maria
Maria has an insecure-avoidant attachment style and

adapts herself so much to her partner that she herself becomes invisible and the relationship runs out in the sand. Maria needed to become aware of her own desire and then learn to express it. She made a situation analysis, as described in Chapter 7, and decided to use the Do-the-Opposite method in situations where she normally put the partner's wishes ahead of her own. This proved, however, to be difficult in the relationship she was already in, and after a while the relationship ended. A few months later Maria met a new man and this time right from the start she took the opportunity to break her old pattern of always trying to please.

She started with apparently trivial situations. In previous relationships when she'd rented a movie with her partner, she always let him choose the movie, even if that led to her being forced to see films she didn't think were interesting. Maria experienced a strong inner resistance to making suggestions, but thanks to the Car Ride tool, complemented by the Willingness tool, she could put up with the difficult emotions and complete the experiment a few times. The result at first was that she and the partner compromised by each renting a movie, which by itself was progress. But gradually Maria learned to pursue her own preferences. She could see with some surprise that her boyfriend accepted this without a problem.

Maria then tried to express her opinions in more important contexts. For a while she felt like a sulky teenager who said no to most things. But gradually she realized that she didn't need to say no to everything, simply because she knew what she wanted herself. When she experimented with sometimes accepting others' wishes, it felt much better than before because she now was making a conscious sacrifice, rather than almost compulsively giving in.

Today Maria is living in a relationship and she finds that it is more exciting and stimulating than any she's had before. At the moment, she feels much less worried about not being good enough.

Lena

Lena has an insecure-ambivalent attachment style. She is governed by emotions, can sometimes be clingier than she wants and then demands guarantees that she won't be abandoned. This sometimes scares away the people she dates.

Lena needs to train herself to stay in the present moment and not let the fear of being abandoned take her several years forward in her thoughts. She started by doing a situation analysis and in that way found situations where she might experiment with doing the opposite. In certain situations she also benefited from the Little Person and Big Person tool to avoid being carried away by her catastrophic thoughts.

The real breakthrough for Lena, however, was that she spent a considerable amount of time training herself in Mindfulness (Chapter 9). After a few weeks of daily training, she experienced a clearly increased capacity to observe her worry with a certain distance. This experience motivated her to continue meditating.

Today Lena has a partner. She can still be affected by strong worry that the relationship will end, but she has a completely different ability to handle this worry than before. For one thing, she knows that regular meditation makes her more stable and secure. For another, she has gotten good at telling her partner about her worry instead of letting suspicion lead to isolation as she did so often before.

Johan

Johan has an insecure-ambivalent attachment style and is governed by emotions. He has had long-term relationships, but can doubt for years whether he's met the right person.

Johan realized that he had to use the Do-the-Opposite method in order to simply stop acting outhis doubt. He made the radical decision not to discuss his thoughts about separation with his girlfriend for at least two years.

In the beginning, two years felt like an endlessly long time and he didn't think he would manage it. Thoughts and emotions were galloping inside him, and his doubts about the relationship became stronger than ever. But by using the Car Ride tool, he succeeded in distancing himself so much from his doubts that he could keep them under control. After a few months he started to realize that scenes and quarrels with his girlfriend were no longer part of their everyday life, and it felt pretty nice to avoid that behavior.

As this is written, a year has passed and Johan says that he seldom thinks about what will happen when the time period is over. Sometimes the thought comes up that perhaps he's with the wrong person, but this feels increasingly foreign. The fact that Johan did something about his problem also means that he and his girlfriend are closer to one another than ever before.

Gustav

Gustav has an insecure-avoidant attachment style, jumping between brief contacts, and can barely stick around until morning.

Gustav needed to train himself in staying put. He used the Little Person and Big Person tool to reveal his concealed longing for security. Then he decided to use the Do-the-Opposite method. His exercise became to try to spend the night with a partner without having sex, and in addition to see the same partner again.

At first it didn't go well. Gustav went home with a woman and succeeded in being content with hugging a little, but early in the morning he got his usual feelings of panic and found himself standing on the sidewalk without really knowing what had just happened. He continued to experiment, however.

The change came about by chance that one morning he overslept at home with a woman he'd met the evening before. When he woke up she had gone to work and left a note saying that she would really like to see him again. While Gustav remained lying in bed he got the desire to do something that in his opinion was "crazy." He called the woman and suggested that they should have dinner at her apartment after work. She said yes and Gustav felt that something big was about to happen. The result became a relationship that doesn't resemble any Gustav had experienced previously, and he feels more open than ever. Gustav is still in therapy, which he thinks continues to help.

Beatrice

Beatrice has an insecure-ambivalent attachment style

and for a long time could only get interested in unavailable men. She has had several long-term relationships as a mistress, but has grown tired of that role.

Beatrice needed to train herself in entering into a relationship without knowing for sure how it was going to end. She also had to train herself in respecting her own emotional needs.

Beatrice benefited from the Little Person and Big Person tool. By talking with her two inner persons, she succeeded in become more aware of which emotional needs she was denying by only wanting to be with men who had essentially abandoned her in advance.

In order to increase her possibilities for being open when she met available men, she used the Get to Know Your Automatic Thoughts tool (see Chapter 7). This helped her to see that it was her own thoughts that caused single men to seem uninteresting and that the driving force behind these thoughts was fear. By charging up with alternate thoughts before a date, she succeeded in refraining from immediately dismissing the man she was seeing, and the date became more enjoyable than she could have imagined. An unexpected effect of Beatrice's experimentation was that the occupied men who previously stood out as attractive soon became completely uninteresting to her.

Today, Beatrice is single. She is dating quite a bit via the Internet and has hopes of one day finding someone she really likes.

Marcus

Twenty-seven-year-old Marcus has an insecure-avoidant attachment style and withdraws when someone shows interest in him. He avoids meeting people he doesn't know.

Marcus tried the Do-the-Opposite method and decided to start by exposing himself to contact with women in contexts that had nothing to do with relationships. He forgot about going to bars, and after a fair amount of agonizing and hesitation he signed up for a dance course a couple of his friends were taking. There he had the opportunity to use the Get to Know Your Automatic Thoughts tool to notice the thoughts that caused him to worry when he met unfamiliar people. He has continued to be involved in contexts where he meets new people and thinks he's becoming more courageous all the time.

Marcus is still single. His long-term project is to expose himself to new contacts and he is no longer saying no to going to parties. He hopes at some point to be able to do something on his own with a woman he's interested in, but he hasn't quite made it there yet.

FINAL WORDS

Essentially, our relationship model is created so early on that we can't even remember how it happened. Despite this, it affects us every day. It is an echo from our past, and it determines whether we feel happiness when faced with a new contact or if we feel worried and avoid it.

Up to now your relationship model has governed your life without you knowing about it. It has caused you to construct a world around you that looks roughly like your relationship model claims that the world should look. But in reality you are free to form your life into the way you want it. Changing your life may seem like an extremely big project. But your life is made up of a complex web of thoughts, emotions and actions that constantly influence one another. If you made a single change in one place in that web, this change will unavoidably affect the rest of the web too.

What is most decisive is going to be your will to change. By reading this book you have already taken a very important first step. If you take another step, you will find yourself a major stride closer to a lasting relationship.

Egil Linge & Dan Josefsson

Appendix:

QUICK GUIDE TO TOOLS AND TECHNIQUES

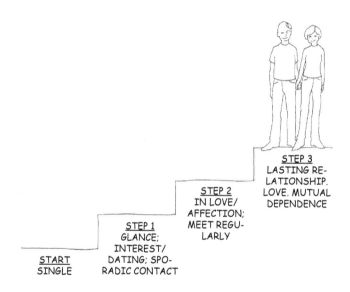

STEP 3
LASTING RE-
LATIONSHIP.
LOVE. MUTUAL
DEPENDENCE

STEP 2
IN LOVE/
AFFECTION;
MEET REGU-
LARLY

STEP 1
GLANCE;
INTEREST/
DATING; SPO-
RADIC CONTACT

START
SINGLE

Do-the-Opposite Method
Step 1: Find a situation and analyze it (see Chapter 6)

Situation Analysis

1.	Problematic situation	
2.	What do you think?	
3.	What do you feel?	
4.	What do you do?	
5.	Short-term benefit	
6.	Long-term consequence	

Step 2: Look at the fourth box. Experiment with intentionally doing the opposite of what you wrote in this box the next time you find yourself in a similar situation.

The Car Ride Tool
When you do the opposite, many thoughts and emotions are going to arise. See the whole experience as a car ride, where your thoughts and emotions are treacherous road signs that you read with interest but do not obey.

The Willingness Tool
Step 1: Imagine that you have a meter that shows how strong your mental pain is (for example in the form of

worry, dissatisfaction, restlessness, skeptical thoughts, or fear). Remember that it is impossible to try using will power to force mental pain to subside because then it just gets stronger.

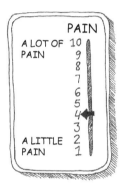
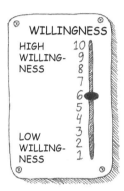

Step 2: Turn over the pain meter. On the back is the regulator that determines your degree of willingness. When you feel a strong need to revert to a behavior that you want to try to leave behind, check that your willingness is at the top. Then you'll be able to manage the troublesome emotions you're feeling at the moment a little better.

Try increasing your degree of willingness in various situations and see what happens.

Get to Know Your Automatic Thoughts Tool

1. Analyze a situation and describe it by filling in the six boxes at the left of the form below.

2. Look at the second box. Question the truth content and reasonableness of the thought.
3. Look for alternative thoughts and write those in Box Two at the right. Investigate what emotions your alternative thoughts might create and describe these in Box Three in the right-hand column. Then think about what actions your alternative thought might lead to. Describe the alternative action in the third box at the right.
4. Experiment with thinking your alternative thought the next time you find yourself in the situation and see what happens.

	Situation Analysis	Alternative
Situation		
What do you think?		
What do you feel?		
What do you do?		
Short-term benefit		
Long-term con-sequence		

Little Person and Big Person Tool

Imagine that you have two versions of yourself inside you: a big version and a little one. The big person takes care of your thoughts and the needs you can think your way to, while the little person takes care of your emotions and the needs that are connected with emotions.

When you are faced with a problematic situation, ask the two persons to comment on the situation.

The Mindfulness Tool
Mindfulness is too big a concept to be summarized in a few lines. Instead read Chapter 9 in its entirety one more time.

Acknowledgments

Egil wants to thank:
All my clients who have given me invaluable knowledge about the mystery of relationships, and my life partner Nina who always stands by my side with love and inspiration.

Dan wants to thank:
Susanne for the illustrations and for all the work you did improving the book. Miranda for showing me how the miracle of connection looks in practice. Hampus Josefsson, Tor Wennerberg, Håkan Linder and Max Wahlund for reading the book at various stages and giving me ideas for improvement. Viktoria Ohlmarker for your encouraging acclaim.

Printed in Great Britain
by Amazon